THE ODYSSEY COOKBOOK

THE ODYSSEY COOKBOOK

"A Culinary Cruise"

by Malcolm R. Hébert

Published by The Wine Appreciation Guild

Other books published by The Wine Appreciation Guild:

THE CHAMPAGNE COOKBOOK
EPICUREAN RECIPES OF CALIFORNIA WINEMAKERS
GOURMET WINE COOKING THE EASY WAY
FAVORITE RECIPES OF CALIFORNIA WINEMAKERS
WINE COOKBOOK OF DINNER MENUS
EASY RECIPES OF CALIFORNIA WINEMAKERS
THE POCKET ENCYCLOPEDIA OF CALIFORNIA WINE
IN CELEBRATION OF WINE AND LIFE
WINE CELLAR RECORD BOOK
CORKSCREWS: An Introduction to Their Appreciation
THE CALIFORNIA WINE DRINK BOOK
THE CALIFORNIA BRANDY DRINK BOOK
NEW ADVENTURES IN WINE COOKERY
WINE IN EVERYDAY COOKING

Published by:

The Wine Appreciation Guild
1377 Ninth Avenue
San Francisco, CA 94122
(415) 566-3532
(415) 957-1377

Library of Congress Catalog Number:
ISBN 0-932664-43-1
Printed in The United States of America
Designed by: Colonna, Caldewey, Farrell; Designers
Illustrations: Susan Bard
Editor: Donna Bottrell
Contributing Editors: Walter Meyer, Ronna Nelson

"And so, these few days while you're on my ship, please make yourself at home. From my officers, my crew and my cruise staff . . . Bon Voyage."

THE CAPTAIN

ACKNOWLEDGEMENTS

Duncan Beardsley, Royal Cruise Line
Laurie R. Chase, Laurie Chase & Co.
Charles Daly, editorial
Walter Meyer, Royal Cruise Line
Dionysios Milatos, Chief Steward aboard the Golden Odyssey
Dan Mirassou, Mirassou Vineyards
Christos Moulas, Royal Cruise Line Executive Chef
P. S. Panagopoulos, Chairman of the Board, Royal Cruise Line
Richard Revnes, President, Royal Cruise Line

TABLE OF CONTENTS

Our floating Hotel

Introduction

Welcome Aboard

There's a special magic once you board a ship.

It's hard to place your finger on it. It's tough to pin down. But it is there. For once you cross that gangway, you feel it. You sense it. And, you taste it.

What is a cruise?

It is anything and everything you want it to be.

It is a walk on the deck under the moonlight where you watch millions of stars play peek-a-boo with you, a hot cup of bouillon that soothes an early morning chill, a bottle of wine that perfectly matches the chef's creation, a priceless color picture of the Leaning Tower of Pisa, Istanbul's Blue Mosque or the medieval city of Dubrovnik, a walk down a cobble-stoned street where Napoleon once marched, a buffet lunch that boasts 26 different choices, a sip of the same old brandy that Winston Churchill once favored, a spin of the roulette wheel at Monte Carlo's world famous Casino and a visit to Bethlehem, the birthplace of Jesus, slip through the locks of the Panama Canal and smell the sweet perfume of the Caribbean.

To others a cruise is a hug, a handshake and a hurrah. It is the meeting of new friends, discovering the way other people live, dressing up for special events and parties, buying any number of rare and unique gifts for relatives and friends. It is a statue standing in the evening sunset which looks as if the sculptor had just finished it, or a midnight snack to quench a sudden hunger. It could be the haunting chant of the monks in a monastery as they sing in Gregorian cadence, the feeding of the thousands of pigeons in St. Mark's Square as they swarm around you, the feeling of history as you stand in the Parthenon, to tread in the very square in Leningrad where Stalin pledged cooperation with the United States, a cruise is many things to many people. It just depends upon what you want.

The history of cruising isn't a modern tale as some people would have you believe. The modern day cruise was born some 91 years ago on January 22, 1891 when the 8,000 ton Augusta Victoria owned by Albert Ballin of Hamburg-Amerika Lines sailed on a pleasure junket around the Mediterranean. It was not only successful, but set a precedent for which today's industry should be forever indebted. His decision to use ships in the off season was innovative and logical and showed that idle ships pressed into service in the off season could produce new revenues. Needless to say, other lines followed Ballin's history making idea.

Packaged for the idle rich and socially prominent, the earliest cruises made a great deal of sense for no others had the financial resources to spend on pleasure ship excursions.

Cruises as we know them today began in the prosperous 1920's even though they were on a grand scale and for a very small segment of society. Transatlantic sailings assumed the importance that world cruises do today. Staterooms were as large as drawing rooms and boasted hand carved furniture. If you traveled first class (and there are some modern day voyagers who insist that first class is still the only way to travel), you traveled with trunks laden with evening clothes and jewels. Servants (many the personal valets and maids of the passengers themselves) were at hand to cater to your every wish.

Cruising today, which is all year long, is far more comfortable than it ever was, despite somewhat smaller staterooms and the lack of personal servants. Ships are physically maintained on a daily basis, and certainly passengers are better cared for by the personal service of the stewards.

Today's cruise ships are floating resorts, featuring pools, live entertainment, gyms, sauna baths, movie theaters, libraries, restaurants, casinos, bars, lectures, golf, tennis, closed circuit television and just plain "doing nothing."

There is no packing and unpacking at each port of call, no traffic jams to and from various airports and no frantic last minute search for accommodations. On today's cruise ships, being there is all the fun.

FROM A MASTER STORYTELLER

"Somerset Maugham once told me that the only place where he felt completely relaxed was aboard ship. As soon as the soft trembling under his feet indicated that they were off and the people and their problems were receding into a haze, there was a wonderful feeling of being lost in time and space."

Joseph Wechsberg,
"The First Time Around,"
Little Brown & Co., 1970

13

The Golden Odyssey

Soups

There is no better way to start a meal than to begin with soup.

Of course there are some people who insist that hors d'ouevres should be served first and then a soup, but I come from the school that suggests, especially on a cruise, soup is the best first course.

It must have been a thrill for early humans to be able to heat water with a bone in it, put it on a fire and in a little while taste a warm and nourishing broth that took away the chills of the day. The soups became thicker and richer as more and more ingredients were added. Soon the soup was so thick that it became the main course, rather than a first course.

The first eating establishment to be called a restaurant was opened in Paris by a Parisian soup vendor, M. Boulanger in 1765 and he served exclusively soups to his clientele. The term "restaurant" is said to have come from M. Boulanger's insistence that his soups had restorative properties.

Queen Elizabeth I and Queen Victoria were fond of sipping a bowl of mutton broth at breakfast because it woke up their appetites. And breakfast soups were popular with Ignace Paderewski and Leopold Stokowski. The Italian composer Guiseppe Verdi attributed much of his inspiration to the warming and sustaining effects of a large bowl of soup.

Since time immemorial country people have kept the stockpot simmering all day long on the kitchen stove, only to be consumed that night and then started all over again the next morning. During periods of disaster and stress, it was the soup kitchens that kept people and countries alive.

Most gourmets claim that they consider soup making to be the ultimate accomplishment of the chef. If this is true, then welcome aboard an Odyssey to sip and savor some of the fine soups Chef Moulas and his chefs have prepared for you.

Soup's on!

Chilled Fruit Borsche with Red Wine

2 lbs. mixed fruit (apple, melon) diced into 1/2 inch pieces
1 lb. black grapes or 1/2 cup grape juice
1/2 bottle red wine
1/2 cup grenadine syrup

Peel and slice the fruit and put it into a large bowl. Slice the grapes in two and remove the seeds. Pour in the wine and grenadine. Blend well. Chill in the refrigerator until very cold. Serves 10.

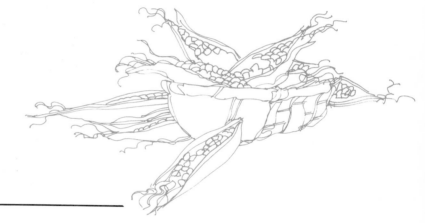

Washington Cream Soup

When Odyssey passengers find themselves at sea on Washington's birthday, they are surprised with:

3 medium sized ears of corn
8 cups chicken stock
4 egg yolks
1/2 cup milk
1/2 cup heavy cream (whipping)
Minced parsley

Cook the ears of corn in boiling water for three minutes. Cool the corn and cut off the kernels. Reserve. Heat the stock in a medium size pot. In a separate bowl beat the yolks, milk and cream and slowly add it to the hot soup. Now add the corn, mix well. Serve hot. Serves 8.

17

Cream of Celery Soup Lisette

REALLY OLD

There are some culinary creations that gastronomic historians cannot trace their origin. One of the oldest is:

a. Salads
b. Wine vinegars
c. Desserts
d. Soups

a. It's salads. Their origin is lost in history. But not on the Odyssey, where the chefs have hundreds for you to choose from for a pleasurable cruise.

The next time you see the following soup on the menu, I suggest you ask for it. You will be in for a nice dinner treat.

1/4 cup peanut oil
1 large onion
2 medium potatoes
1 whole celery heart
2 medium carrots
1 Tbs. flour
8 cups beef stock
4 egg yolks
1/2 cup heavy cream
6 Tbs. butter

Heat the oil in a large pot and add the vegetables which have been peeled and sliced into small pieces, except for the celery heart. Stir for a few minutes and then add the flour and the stock. Bring to the boil and cook until the vegetables are soft. Put the cooked vegetables and their liquid into a blender or food processor. Put the blended mixture into a pot and put it on simmer. In separate bowl beat the eggs, milk and cream and add to the liquid mixture. Cut the celery heart into small cubes and boil for two minutes. Add the hearts to the soup along with the butter. Bring to the boil. Serve hot. Serves 6.

Christmas Consomme

Here is a simple soup that can be and is served on an Odyssey around the Christmas season. However, with enough notice, the ship's chefs will be happy to prepare it for you and your fellow passengers at any time.

6 whole eggs
2 cups whole milk
Salt and pepper to taste
4 gratings fresh nutmeg
6 cups consomme
30 boiled asparagus tips, fresh or frozen

Beat the eggs, milk, salt, pepper and nutmeg together in a bowl. Place the mixture in a flat bowl and cook the mixture over hot water in a low oven, never letting the water come to the boil. When the mixture thickens, take it out and cut it into 1/2 inch cubes. Divide the asparagus tips evenly among six soup bowls. Add eight pieces of the cubed egg squares and add the hot consomme to each of the six bowls. Serve hot. Serves 6.

DRILL RIGHT

International regulations require all passengers take part in a boat drill at least once during the cruise. Life jackets are found in the closets of each stateroom. The time and date for the boat drill will be given in the Daily Program and announced over the loudspeaker system.

19

Avoglemono Soup

GULP!

The French king, Louis XIV was a gourmet. He was also an insatiable gourmand. He ate, as a rule, three soups, five entrees, five fowls, two fish and vegetable dishes. In addition, he tasted various roasts, shellfish, desserts, eggs, a few salads, fruits and nibbled on anything that pleased his palate. All of this was consumed at a single meal.

One of the oldest of all soups is the Greek soup, Avoglemono. And it is one of the best soups you can begin a meal with and not feel stuffed. Here is the authentic version, just for you.

2 cups chicken stock
2 cups beef stock
1/2 cup uncooked rice
3 egg yolks
Juice of two medium lemons
1/4 to 1/2 tsp. cornstarch (optional)

Combine stock and bring to the boil. Add rice and cook until fluffy. Beat yolks until frothy and add lemon juice. Slowly blend into the egg mixture 2 to 3 tablespoons of the hot stock. Add mixture to the hot soup stirring constantly. If you want a thicker soup, mix the cornstarch with cold water and add it to the soup. Serves 4.

Cream of Leek Soup

One of the oldest soups in the world is one of the simplest to make. It utilizes one of the best tasting members of the onion family, the leek.

2 medium potatoes, diced
2 medium leeks, diced, white part only
6 cups chicken stock
2 cups heavy cream (whipping)

Cook the potatoes and leeks in the stock over low heat until the potatoes are soft. Puree the mixture in a blender or food processor. Pour into a pot and add the cream. Heat to the boil. Serve hot. Serves 6.

ODYSSEY SECRET: Wash the green leek tops and cut them into two inch pieces. Shred them very fine and sprinkle on top of the soup.

Borscht

No menu on a cruise ship that visits Leningrad would be complete without a recipe for Russian Borscht. Here is a hearty soup that should be served very hot.

8 large beets, peeled and halved
2 lbs. beef stew meat, cut into 2-inch squares, bones too
1 cup canned stewed tomatoes
3 quarts water
1 good sized cabbage, shredded
1 apple, peeled and quartered
2 tsps. salt
1 tsp. fresh ground black pepper
1 - 15 oz. can lima beans

1/2 pint sour cream

In a deep soup kettle, combine the beets, meat, bones, tomatoes and water, bring to the boil and skim the top. Cook for 1-1/2 hours over medium heat. Add cabbage, apple, salt and pepper. Cook 30 minutes more. With a slotted spoon remove the beets, and grate them. Return beets to soup. To serve, make sure the bones are removed. Divide the meat evenly among the portions and top each bowl with a large dollop of sour cream. Serves 10.

Turkish Wedding Soup

There is a great deal of dancing and singing and eating at a Turkish wedding. Like many occasions, a wedding is a festive meeting place where all the families gather to celebrate with the newlyweds. One of the great dishes always served at a Turkish nuptial is a special wedding soup, rich and sustaining. It is probably served to make sure the groom can withstand the continuous eating and drinking during the day long celebration. It is served on the Odyssey because the passengers continue to ask for it.

3 lbs. lamp stew meat
1 large onion, peeled
1 large carrot, peeled
1/8 tsp. Cayenne pepper
2-1/2 quarts water
4 Tbs. butter
4 Tbs. flour
3 egg yolks
3 Tbs. fresh lemon juice
5 Tbs. melted butter
1/2 tsp. Paprika

Put the first five ingredients into a soup kettle and bring to the boil. Cover and cook gently over low heat for 3 hours. Melt the 4 tablespoons of butter and mix with the flour to make a paste. Slowly add paste to the soup stirring constantly. Cook slowly for 15 minutes. Meanwhile beat yolks with lemon juice and slowly add 2 cups of the hot soup. Return egg mixture to the soup, stirring. DO NOT LET THE SOUP BOIL AFTER THE EGGS HAVE BEEN ADDED. Add a spoonful of the melted butter to each portion and top with the Paprika. Serves 6.

Cream Soup Eleonora

Here is another soup that is a favorite with Odyssey passengers. Once you taste it, it might become your favorite too.

1/4 cup oil
1 large onion, diced
2 medium potatoes, peeled and diced
1/2 cup celery, diced
2 carrots, peeled and diced
1 Tb. flour
8 cups of beef broth
4 egg yolks
1/2 cup whole milk
1/2 cup heavy cream (whipping)
2 Tbs. butter
1/2 lb. boiled lamb, cut into small cubes
1 cup boiled rice

In a large saucepan heat the oil and cook the vegetables for 5 minutes, stirring frequently. Add flour and broth, bring to the boil and cook until the vegetables are soft. Puree in the blender or food processor. Return to the pan and cook on the simmer for another 10 minutes. In a separate bowl, beat the yolks, milk and cream and add to the soup stirring constantly. Now add lamb, rice and butter, stir well and serve very hot. Serves 8.

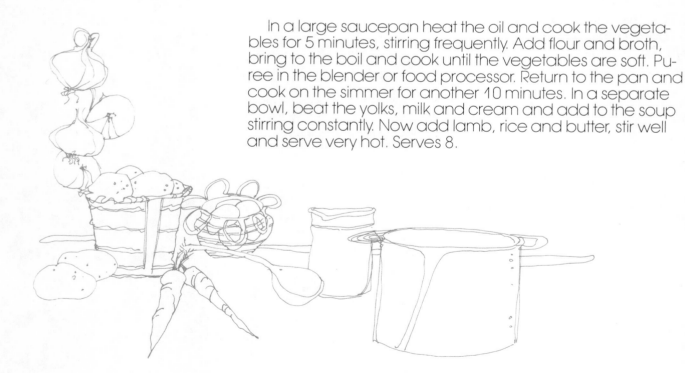

Through the Panama Canal

How To Talk
Like An Old Salt

SHIP SHAPE

They are called ships. If you slip and say "boat", there are several hundred people who will correct you.

It's a ship.
Like in "ship" shape.
So, shape up.
Say "ship".

A ship is always referred to in the female gender. The reason, so an old story goes, is because "she shows her topside, hides her bottom and when coming into port she heads for the buoys."

There are some 5,000 words in the special language of the sea, and the first time you take a cruise, Neptune's dialect is apt to confuse you. But don't fret, many a sea-faring sailor has taken a few months to catch on to the terminology of Davy Jones' locker.

And there is no need to increase your vocabulary so that every other word you speak is nautical. But you should know the everyday terms used by the crew and knowledgeable passengers. It helps you to enjoy the cruise because you have become a part of the gang.

So here are some of the most often used words, nautical terms, that is, plus a few more.

As to the ship herself, the front of the ship is called the **bow,** while the rear of the ship is called the **stern.** If you walk toward the bow you are walking **forward,** while toward the stern is **aft.** If you stand in the middle of the ship, you are **amidships.**

When you face the bow of the ship, the left side of the ship is the **port** side and the right side is the **starboard** side. ODYSSEY SECRET: If you forget port and starboard, remember that the port side of the ship has a red navigational light while the starboard side has a green navigational light.

If you like the wind in your face you will be **windward,** while the side out of the wind is the **lee** side. And you should know that the width of the ship is called the **beam** and the depth below the waterline is the **draft.**

No matter where you walk on the Odyssey, every floor you walk on is not a floor, but a **deck.** As you move about, you

must remember that you do not go downstairs, you go **below.** And if you decide to go outside on the ship, you are going **topside,** which also means the decks above the **main deck,** the highest deck running all the way from the front to the back . . . oops . . . from the bow to the stern.

Don't call them stairs, even though at your house you call them that: on a ship they are called **ladders.** And those walls that space off everything on the ship aren't walls, they are **bulkheads.**

The speed of a ship is measured in **knots,** which translated into laymen's terms is about 1-1/6 land miles per hour.

The captain's domain, the ship's command center, is called the **bridge.** Here is where all the navigational decisions are made to make sure that you have a smooth cruise. Passengers are seldom admitted, for the business of running the ship is a very serious undertaking; however, a special tour can sometimes be managed with the Cruise Director.

The captain steers the ship by using the **helm.** If the ship is moving it is **underway;** if the ship is moving backwards, she is going **astern** and that frothy water she leaves behind is the **wake.**

As the ship sails the seas, its motion from side to side means she's **rolling** while the motion fore and aft — when the bow rises and falls — means she's **pitching.** And when the ship leans to one side or the other, she's not at a tilt, but a **heel** or **list.**

You board a ship on a **gangway,** dine on food cooked in a **galley,** tie up your ship with **lines** and tie up at a **pier** or **wharf** because a dock, say old time sailors, is water space between piers.

That's about all the nautical lingo you'll need to know.

Steady as she goes!

Dining in the Grand Manner

Meat

SAY WAITER . . .

You'll never go hungry on an Odyssey cruise.

Passengers have been known to enjoy eight meals in one day: early morning coffee and rolls by the pool, continental breakfast in their stateroom, full American breakfast in the restaurant, mid-morning bouillon, a deck buffet served poolside, luncheon in the restaurant, dinner and a midnight buffet snack.

Still hungry? Well, the Odyssey offers a 24-hour room service with a variety of snacks.

And the nice part about all this is it is included in your cruise fare.

No matter how you slice it, meat is one of man's favorite dishes. The discovery of fire did more to advance the consumption of meat than the cornucopia of animals that roamed the world.

It is the American Indian that you and I have to thank for the way we eat today. The Pilgrims landed on a shore whose waters were teeming with a multitude of various fish, but they were listless fishermen; they were surrounded by forests full of game, but they were indifferent hunters; the land on which they settled was fertile, but they were indifferent farmers. The Indians taught the Pilgrims how to become sophisticated farmers and excellent cooks.

The American Indian has made a very significant contribution to American cuisine. We owe the American Indian the clambake, roasted peanuts, cranberry sauce, clam chowder, codfish cakes, Boston baked beans, pumpkin soup, Brunswick stew, et cetera.

While the Pilgrims and the Indians were helping each other with developing an American cuisine, the French about that same time were planning the following summer dinner for fifteen people according to "La Cuisiniere Bourgeoise," the first modern cookbook, published about 1770.

The menu begins:

Place a large roast beef in the center of the table.

FIRST SERVICE — cucumber soup, green pea soup, fried mutton feet, veal roast in pastry, small patés and melons.

SECOND SERVICE — boiled leg of mutton, roast veal marinated in cream, duckling with peas, squab with herbs, two chickens with little white onions and rabbit steaks with cucumbers.

THIRD SERVICE — Replace the roast beef with a large brioche, one small turkey, one capon, four partridges, six squabs roasted like quail and two green salads.

FOURTH SERVICE — apricot tartlets, scrambled eggs, vine leaf fritters, cookies, small white beans and artichokes with butter sauce.

FIFTH SERVICE — large fresh fruit bowl, peaches, prunes, pears, green grapes, plates of ice cream, cream cheese and pastries.

Veal Scaloppini a la Monte Carlo

I have said before that the cuisine aboard the Odyssey is international and this veal scaloppini dish fits perfectly into the ecumenical menu offered by the chef and his staff. In the recipe below, it calls for thin slices of ham: aboard the Odyssey, the ham is the famed Italian prosciutto.

**8 slices of milk fed veal, cut into 4 inch squares and
   pounded thin**
2 Tbs. butter
Salt and pepper to taste
2 cups tomato sauce
8 slices of ham or prosciutto, sliced very thin
8 slices of Provolone cheese, sliced very thin
Paprika

Salt the veal slices in the butter until barely cooked. Put the veal slices in a baking pan, sprinkle with salt and pepper. Top the veal slices with one tablespoon of the tomato sauce, then add a slice of ham and a slice of cheese. Dust with paprika and bake at 325 degrees for 10 minutes. Serves 8.

TASTE TREAT

President Franklin Roosevelt and his wife did a great deal of entertaining when they were in the White House. When King George of England visited the White House, the Roosevelts served them:

   a. Pancakes
   b. Chile
   c. Hot dogs
   d. French food

c. King George and his spouse had never tasted hot dogs.

Roast Baby Lamb a la Roumeli

FAMILY FRIENDS

If you like spices, you should know that anise, caraway, celery seed, chervil, coriander, cummin, dill and fennel all belong to the same family. We know it as:

a. Onion
b. Garlic
c. Parsley
d. Carrot

c. They belong to the parsley family which is believed to be the largest of the herb and spice family.

And if you are looking for a new way to serve your leg or shoulder of lamb, you might try this authentic Odyssey recipe.

3-4 lb. leg or shoulder of lamb
4 cloves garlic, slivered
1 whole lemon, halved
Salt and pepper to taste
1 cup olive oil
1 lb. potatoes, peeled and cut into quarters
1 cup water
2 Tbs. lemon juice
1 tsp. oregano
Hearts of lettuce

Insert the garlic slivers into the lamb. Rub the lamb with the lemon halves, salt and pepper and a little of the oil. Put the meat in a roasting pan, surrounded by the potatoes. Add remaining oil, water and lemon juice, pouring them over the potatoes. Sprinkle with oregano. Bake in a hot oven, about 400 degrees, adding more water if necessary until the meat is done, about 1 to 1-1/2 hours. The potatoes should be nicely browned and have absorbed all the water. Cut the lamb in portions. Put the meat on one side of the plate and the potatoes on the other side of the plate. Garnish with hearts of lettuce. Serves 6.

Beef Boerek

Or if you prefer something different, here is this dish to whet your appetite.

2 large onions, chopped fine
2 Tbs. olive oil
1-1/2 lbs. lean ground beef
Salt and pepper to taste
1 clove garlic, minced
2 Tbs. parsley, minced
1/2 cup pine nuts
6 Tbs. butter, melted
2 eggs
36 sheets filo pastry, 6" by 8"

In one tablespoon of the oil, saute the onions until soft. Place in mixing bowl. In the remaining oil saute the beef, crumbling it with a fork. Add beef to onions. Add salt and pepper, garlic and parsley. Saute the pine nuts in one tablespoon of butter until golden brown and add to mixture. Add eggs. Combine all ingredients until well mixed. Take one filo sheet and cover the remaining with a damp cloth. Brush the filo sheet with the melted butter. Top with a second sheet and brush with butter. Divide the meat mixture into 18 portions. Place one portion of the meat filling on the filo pastry nearest to you. Fold the sides up about one inch. Roll the filo up. Place seam side down on a lightly greased baking dish. Repeat for the remaining filo and filling. Bake the little packages at 400 degrees for 15 minutes. Makes 18 rolls, three per person. Serves 6. NOTE: If you like, you can top it off with the famed Greek sauce, Avgolemono.

Avoglemono Sauce

2 egg yolks
Juice of one large lemon
1 to 2 cups stock (chicken, beef, veal, lamb)

In a mixing bowl whisk the eggs two minutes. Continue to beat the eggs while adding the lemon juice slowly. Then add hot stock by drops and continue adding until the sauce is thick enough to coat the back of a wooden spoon. Yield: 1 cup.

Beef a la Bourguigon

There are many dishes whose origins are hard to trace. The truth has vanished under gossip, storytelling and added emphasis. This is especially true with the notable Boeuf a la Bourguigon, for which there can be as many as a hundred varied interpretations of this classical French entree. There are several stories as to how this dish was created, but I like this one best.

It seems that one day a comely miss accidentally toppled a large bottle of Burgundy wine into the chef's beef stew. Before she could lift the hot bottle out of the pot, almost all of it had spilled into the stew. She told no one about it until that evening when the master of the house sat down to eat and discovered a new taste sensation. He called his chef in to explain what had happened and the chef was at a loss to explain why the beef stew tasted so good. He ranted and raved and finally the little lady told him of the accident. He praised her and told the chef never again to make his favorite stew the old way.

2 Tbs. salad oil
1 cup diced salt pork, blanched
1 cup diced carrots
2 lbs. beef rump or chuck cut into one inch pieces
Salt and pepper to taste
1 clove garlic, chopped
2 medium onions, chopped
2 shallots or scallions, chopped
1/2 lb. mushrooms, sliced
1/2 bottle Burgundy or any red wine
1/3 cup cognac or California brandy

In a deep skillet or large pan, pour in the salad oil. Add half the salt pork, all the diced carrots, cover with 1/3 of the beef cubes. Sprinkle with salt and pepper. Then sprinkle evenly with half the onions, garlic, shallots and mushrooms. Cover this layer with half the remaining beef. Add salt and pepper. Add remaining onions, shallots, garlic and mushrooms. Cover with remaining beef and salt pork. Pour in Burgundy and brandy. Cook on high heat until the mixture boils, then lower heat and simmer for 2-1/2 to 3 hours. Serves 6.

Filet of Beef with Truffle Sauce

Ingredients have always played a large part in all cuisines of the world. Curry is Indian in origin. Hot pepper is Spanish as well as Chinese in origin. And brandy is used by almost all countries as a flavor enhancer, a sort of extra essence that raises a dish to voluptuous heights. This dish only uses a half cup of brandy.

1/4 lb. butter (one stick)
6 medium sized beef filets
1-1/2 tsps. salt
1/2 tsp. fresh ground black pepper
4 thin slices of black truffles, minced
1/2 cup brandy
1 cup canned beef stock or homemade beef stock

In a saucepan, melt two tablespoons of butter and saute the steaks over a high heat until you reach the desired degree of rareness. Sprinkle with salt and pepper and place in a slack oven to keep warm. In the same saucepan add the truffles, brandy and stock and reduce the liquid by half. Add remaining butter, stir until melted and pour over filets. Serves 6.

THANKSGIVING SURPRISE

The first Thanksgiving was really a breakfast. But it did end with a special surprise. When the Pilgrims and their ninety plus Indian guests had finished eating, Chief Massasoit's brother, Quadequina, ran into the woods and returned with a bushel of popped popcorn. Needless to say it was a startling novelty to the Pilgrims.

Youvarelakia

A TIP ON TIPPING

There is no mystery about tipping. Aboard the Odyssey, you only have to be concerned about one tip, which goes into a giant fund to be divided amongst the staff. Royal Cruise Line even suggests an amount to alleviate all your possible anxiety.

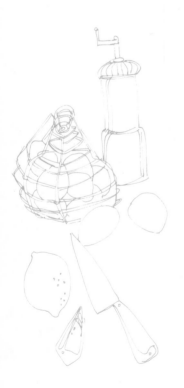

A main course that is extremely popular aboard the Odyssey is one of the easiest to prepare, difficult to pronounce, one that you can prepare at home after your cruise. This dish is very similar to the French dish "quenelles" which is served with a white sauce. Here, the Odyssey chefs use a lemon and egg sauce.

2 lbs. minced meat from either beef, pork or veal
2 onions, grated
3 Tbs. chopped dill
1 Tb. chopped mint
1 cup bread crumbs
3 eggs
6 oz. butter
1 cup rice
1/2 cup water
Salt and pepper to taste

In a mixing bowl blend together the meat, onion, dill, mint, crumbs, eggs and half the butter. Scald the rice in the water for five minutes and add to the mixture along with the salt and pepper. Leave the mixture in a cool place for 30 minutes. Now shape the mixture in round balls about the size of a small egg. Lay them on the bottom of a large sauce pan and barely cover with boiling water, pouring carefully from the side so as to not break the balls. Add the remaining butter, press each ball slightly, cover and simmer for 30 to 45 minutes.

Lemon Egg Sauce

2 eggs
Juice of 2 lemons
2 Tbs. water
1 oz. butter, melted
1 cup of broth from the above recipe

Beat eggs with lemon juice, water, butter until well mixed. Slowly add the hot broth stirring with a whisk and mix until thick. Pour over meat balls. Serves 6.

Veal "Kapama" Athenis Style

If you are into casserole cooking with a Greek accent, here is one of the Odyssey's best foot forward.

2 lbs. veal, cut into 1/2 inch cubes
1 cup olive oil
1 grated onion
3 cloves garlic, minced
1 Tb. flour
1/2 cup white wine
1 lb. ripe tomatoes, peeled, seeded and chopped
1/2 cup tomato paste
2 cups water
Salt and pepper to taste
2 lbs. string beans, fresh or frozen

Saute the veal in a casserole in the oil with the onion and garlic, making sure that the meat is brown all over. Add remaining ingredients, except green beans, and cook the mixture for 30 minutes over low heat. Push the meat to one side and add the beans. Cover and cook another 20 minutes over medium heat. Serves 6.

Lucullus Veal Youretsi

One of the first orders of cruise protocol is to select your dining arrangements. Aboard the Odyssey there are two seatings for you to choose from: main seating and late seating — for dinner this means 6:30 PM or 8:30 PM.

If you advise Royal Cruise Line of your personal preference when you make your reservation, they will make every effort to accommodate you.

The ancient Roman, Lucullus, was one of the first apostles of the gourmet life. He was so involved in gastronomic delights that he instructed his chef and servants to spend $1,000 per person, per dinner. Nothing was to be spared for the special guests of Lucullus.

One evening, after a long and hard day in the Roman Senate, Lucullus decided to dine alone at his villa. The meal was glorious, but as the dinner progressed, Lucullus discovered that his chef had spent much less than the usual $1,000 per person. He called his chef and demanded to know why he had violated the specific rules Lucullus had set down for gourmet dining.

Confused, the chef sought to explain it away with, "But, Master, since you were dining alone . . ."

Lucullus exploded. "This is why dinner is to be extra special. Lucullus is the guest of Lucullus."

Lucullus was right when he made that statement. If one dines alone, she or he is the guest of herself or himself. Too often we lose sight of the fact that just because we dine alone we shouldn't let things slip; the china doesn't have to be just right, the napkins are a little frayed, we really don't need candlelight, and maybe the wine . . .

Not so aboard the Odyssey. There are many chances to dine with your friends or dine alone with your loved one, and each time everything is just right. The ghost of Lucullus stands ready to let you be the guest of yourself. Next time aboard, try:

2 lbs. veal, cut into 1/2 inch cubes
Salt and pepper to taste
5 Tbs. butter
2 cloves garlic, chopped
2 lbs. tomatoes, peeled, seeded and chopped
4 cups chicken stock
1/2 lb. thin macaroni
1/2 lb. Feta cheese, cut in small cubes

Lucullus Veal Youretsi (cont.)

Rub the veal with the salt and pepper. In a roasting pan or casserole put the meat, 2 Tbs. of butter, the garlic, and tomatoes and bake in a 325 degree oven for 30 minutes. Add the stock, bring to the boil and add the macaroni. Stir frequently to keep the macaroni from sticking. If it appears to be too dry add more stock. When the macaroni is half way cooked, add the feta cheese and remaining butter. Simmer for another 10 minutes. Serves 8.

Veal Chef Moulas

Sometimes the simple dishes of a country are the best. These are the dishes that can be called the "staples" of a country, because they never die and always seem to taste better and better. Many such dishes are served aboard the Odyssey.

2 lbs. veal cut into one inch pieces
4 cloves garlic, minced
1/2 cup olive oil
Juice of 1/2 large lemon
1 tsp. salt
1/2 tsp. white pepper
1 tsp. dried oregano
2 lbs. small potatoes, peeled and diced
1 lb. fresh tomatoes, peeled, seeded and chopped

Marinate the veal in the garlic, oil, lemon juice, salt, pepper and oregano, for 10 to 15 minutes in a large bowl. Add the potatoes and tomatoes. Mix well. Pour the mixture into a butter baking dish and bake at 350 degrees for one hour. Serves 4.

Dolmathes 1

HOW TO STUFF A GRAPE LEAF

Almost as famous as Greek brandy are the grape leaves from the vines that produce it! By making a simple meat-and-rice stuffing and rolling it in the grape leaves, I have an economical and delicious gourmet snack. Most food stores have canned grape leaves.

The more I study about foods and wines, the more I am inclined to see great parallels weaving their way through all cuisines. Take the Greek Dolmathes, which are stuffed grape leaves or cabbage leaves. In German cuisine, instead of using grape or cabbage leaves, they used pounded meat and stuffing; and roll them up.

The French use chicken breasts, pounded thin and stuff them with a savory mixture, roll them up and cook them. They call them "little birds without heads." The Chinese use large fresh lettuce leaves, moisten them with Hoisin sauce and stuff them with minced squab. The Swiss use cabbage leaves and wrap shrimp in the leaves; the Italians have their Bocconcini which are veal scaloppini wrapped around a meat stuffing; the list is endless.

1 lb. lean ground beef
1 egg, beaten
1 medium onion, finely chopped
1/2 cup raw rice
1/4 cup snipped parsley
1 tsp. crushed fresh mint leaves or 1/2 tsp. dried mint
2 Tbs. olive oil
1-3/4 cups water
Salt and pepper to taste
Grape leaves, fresh or canned
1-1/2 cups canned beef bouillon
Avgolemono Sauce

Mix beef and egg. Add onion, rice, parsley, mint, olive oil, 1/4 cup water. Season to taste with salt, pepper. If using fresh grape leaves soak in hot water for 5 minutes to soften. If canned, rinse leaves in warm water. To stuff a grape leaf (see illustration) put it on your work surface shiny side down, stem toward you. Place spoonful of meat mixture on leaf near stem end. Using both hands, fold leaf up and over filling. Roll, folding ends as you go to seal in mixture. Place folded side down in saucepan, making more than 1 layer if necessary. Add bouillon and remaining water. Cover. Simmer 45 minutes. Makes 4 to 6 servings. Serve with Avgolemono Sauce.

Dolmathes 2

Dolmathes are a double duty dish. They can be served as a hors d'oureves or as a main course. The first recipe uses grape leaves and is served as an hors d'oureves while the second recipe uses cabbage leaves and is served as a main course.

1-3 lb. cabbage
2 lbs. minced meat, veal, pork or lamb
1 chopped onion
1/2 cup rice
2 Tbs. chopped dill
5 eggs
1 cup of bread, wet in water and squeezed dry
Salt and pepper to taste
3 cups water
2 Tbs. lemon juice
2 Tbs. cornstarch

Boil the cabbage head until the leaves are tender. Drain and leave to cool. In a bowl mix the meat, onion, rice, dill, 2 eggs, bread and salt and pepper. Take one tablespoon of the meat mixture and place it in the center of a cabbage leaf. Overlap the corners and roll it up like a ball or small sausage. Then lay the Dolmathes close together in a saucepan. Cover with water and simmer for one hour. Beat the remaining three eggs with the lemon juice and cornstarch and add some liquid from the Dolmathes to make a medium thick sauce. Drain the liquid from the Dolmathes, place Dolmathes on a plate and cover with the sauce. Serves 6.

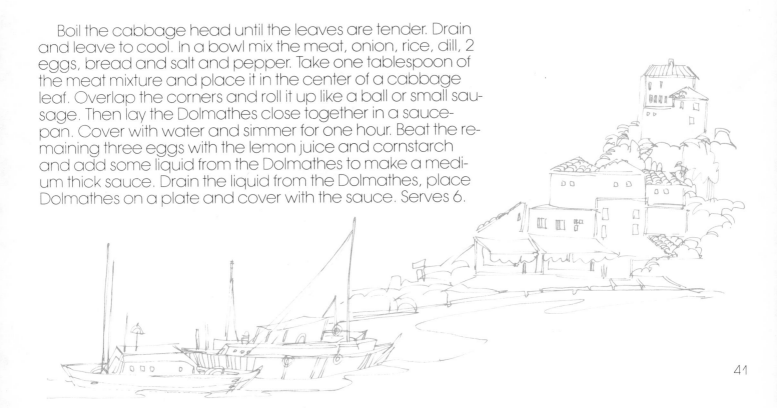

Eggplant & Lamb Casserole

TWO IS ENOUGH

There is only one plant in the entire world that produces two spices from a single plant. You and I know it as:

a. Black & White pepper
b. Fennel & Anise
c. Mace & Nutmeg
d. Garlic & Shallots

c. The fruit looks like an apricot. When ripe, it splits open exposing both the mace and nutmeg.

Here is another such country dish, the kind that has been enjoyed for centuries by the people of the land. Like all great country dishes, this uses the ingredients of the farm.

**1/2 cup salad oil
1 medium eggplant, peeled, sliced into 1/4 inch pieces
2 medium onions, chopped fine
2 lbs. lean ground lamb
2 tsp. salt
1 tsp. fresh ground black pepper
1-2 tsp. ground cinnamon
2 cups cooked rice**

Heat half the oil in a skillet and brown the eggplant on both sides. Remove eggplant and set aside. Add remaining oil to skillet and add remaining ingredients, except rice, cooking them for 10 minutes. Butter a casserole. Arrange a layer of rice on the bottom of the casserole. Now add 1/3 of the lamb mixture. Add a layer of eggplant. Continue making successive layers of rice, lamb and eggplant, ending with the rice on top. Bake 35 minutes in a 375 degree oven or until the top is brown. Serves 6.

Exploring the Ruins

Shopping, Sightseeing, Supping

BOOK AHEAD

Unless you are an experienced traveler, you are better off booking the various excursions the Odyssey has to offer. In the long run it is cheaper, more convenient, and you will have more fun. You will just be able to sit back and enjoy your trip.

Half the fun of a cruise is the shopping, sightseeing and tasting the native foods and wines. Veteran cruise addicts claim that the "cruise lingers on" when you bring gifts to friends and relatives who weren't lucky enough to be with you. It gives you a chance to brag about the wonderful days and nights aboard the Odyssey, plus the discovery of many new and interesting places and ports of call.

There is something enchanting, fascinating and irresistible knowing that the Odyssey is about to drop anchor in a new port, in a place which has an exotic name. It is probably a place that you have always wanted to visit, a place you have thought about wandering down the old hand hewn streets, purchasing that uncommon gift for Aunt Mary and dying to taste a memorable meal with a noted wine. (Of course, you can choose to have all your meals aboard ship.)

If this is what you have been waiting for, look no further. I am going to take you on a "land" cruise and tell you what to see, what to buy and what to eat and drink.

Highlights from the EUROPE / MEDITERRANEAN cruises:

CADIZ, Spain

WHAT TO SEE: This 3,000 year old seaport on the southern apron of the Iberian Peninsula is almost African in appearance with its palm trees, white-washed houses, cupolas and street stalls filled with oranges. From the port of Cadiz you must travel northward to Seville.

WHAT TO BUY: Leather bags, suede jackets, coats and belts along with the Spanish mantillas, flamenco dolls, shawls, fans, castanets, ceramics, tiles and original oil paintings of the Andalusian scenery, are all good buys.

WHAT TO EAT AND DRINK: No matter how much time you have in Seville, you must visit a sherry bar and sip sherry and eat tapas, a happy invention of Spanish dining. Tapas are little canapes and dishes found in almost every bar and hotel. Buy a glass of sherry and the tapas are free. Tapas were invented by the Spanish to hold them over in the evening because they do not eat dinner until 11:00 in the evening.

Tapas to look for include **Lomo,** thin slices of pork filet marinated in Sherry wine and herbs; **Choriza al Inferno,** a spicy Spanish red sausage flamed in Spanish brandy; **Gambas a**

la Plance, grilled and buttered shrimp and **Alcachofas,** artichokes served in a variety of dressings. Other dishes you will see on the menus are **Sopa de Cuarto de Hora,** a delightful fish soup containing mussels, oysters, shrimps, clams, bacon, rice and hard boiled eggs; **Paella a la Valenciana,** a mixture of shellfish, meat and vegetables bathed in saffron coated rice; **Centollos,** minced crabs sauteed in brandy, sherry and tomato sauce stuffed into the shells and dotted with butter. **Capon Relleno a la Catnalena** is a beef, sausage and potato stew cooked in Spanish brandy, red wine and a half dozen herbs. The best desserts are the fresh fruits. And don't forget to taste the various sherries the Spanish make so well.

CIVITAVECCHIA (Rome)

WHAT TO SEE: This is the Eternal City, so named because nothing seems to stop here. It is the seat of one of the most influential religions in the world. It's architecturally and historically one of the great cities of the world and for the sightseer, it offers unlimited views and perspectives. Only 2,400 years old, Rome today is a city that loves tourists. Make sure to see the Vatican and St. Peter's Church; the Sistine Chapel where the paintings of Michelangelo alone are worth an all day trip; walk down the Spanish steps, have coffee on the Via Veneto and visit the Treve Fountain. (NOTE: When you leave the Treve Fountain, turn your back to it and toss a coin into the fountain. The legend says that if you do this, you will return to Rome.) Then there is the Coliseum, Piazza del Popolo, Piazza del Navorna, Piazza Venezia and dozens more to explore.

WHAT TO BUY: The Italians are masters with leather goods for shoes, gloves, purses and pocketbooks. Silk is another Italian specialty for shirts, ties and scarves. Then there are antiques, porcelain and a must visit to the elegant shops of the Via Condotti such as Gucci, Cucci, Valentino and Bulgari.

WHAT TO EAT AND DRINK: If there is one dish that you should try it is **Saltimbocca alla Romano,** composed of paper thin slices of milk fed veal laced with proscuitto and a sage leaf cooked in white wine; **Spaghetti alla Carbonara,** in which spaghetti is tossed with cooked bacon, raw eggs and grated Parmesan cheese; **Bocconcini,** thin slices of veal rolled up with ham and cheese and cooked in butter, and drink the **Frascati wine,** especially from Fontana Candida. It is light, refreshing and drunk all over Rome.

EASY EATING

In the ruling class of Rome in the heyday of the Empire, feasting was a high art. Like the Greeks, the Romans sat on couches around the table with their heads just above the level of the table. They rested on their left elbow and ate with their right hand. The Romans were the first to use napkins.

DAKAR (Senegal)

WHAT TO SEE: The best way to see and enjoy African Dakar is to walk or ride through the busy city. There is the historical and ethnographic museum with its fine collection of West African art. An hour's drive from the city is Cayer, a thatched roofed village. Dakar itself is a melange of old fashioned buildings and modern structures; especially beautiful is the new Dakar Mosque (80% of the Senegalese are Moslem). The Odyssey special tour includes a trip to view some official and private residences.

WHAT TO BUY: For the ladies a colorful (maybe filmy) "boubou" shift and matching turban "moussor". (Men can wear a short boubou with trousers but no headdress!) Also jewelry: silver filagree and gold, beads, sharks teeth, elegant elephant ivory, wonderous woodcarving from the sublime (and portable) to the fantastic (and in size unbearable), "forbidden" crocodile and reptile bags and belts, musical instruments, including the attractive but bulky cora and balafon (xylophone) and the ever present African tam-tam. In most places, the better you bargain, the better the price.

WHAT TO EAT AND DRINK: You are better off dining aboard the Odyssey.

DUBROVNIK (Yugoslavia)

WHAT TO SEE: The open market here is a photographer's dream. It is just behind the Cathedral and near the Rector's Palace. Within the old town your Yugoslavian guides will walk you through ancient history. You might even have time to sip a "slibovich", the traditional plum brandy, before you visit the state controlled shops along the plaka and the narrow streets. For a spectacular view of the city, take the cable car ride above town.

WHAT TO BUY: Wood carvings, leather goods including belts, ladies purses, brief cases and luggage, hand embroidered table mats, blouses, antiques, porcelain and crystal from Eastern Europe.

WHAT TO EAT AND DRINK: Cevapcici, a popular Yugoslav snack composed of grilled meat balls served with minced onions and chilies; **Podvarak,** chopped sour cabbage baked with a whole duckling and pork chops; **Alaska Corbu,** a special fisherman's soup found everywhere; **Jabuke u Rumu,** a dessert of whole apples stewed in rum and sugar. To drink, try the **Fruskogorski Biser,** a white sparkling wine.

LIVORNO (Florence, Pisa) Italy)

WHAT TO SEE: This is the jumping off point to visit two of Italy's greatest cities, Florence and Pisa. Florence houses some of Italy's richest art treasures and this fact is never more awesome as when you stand under Michelangelo's 17 foot David.

WHAT TO BUY: The Florentines are masters with leather, so wallets, purses, handbags, belts, etc. are a must on your shopping list. Other items to consider include hand embroidered linens and silk lingerie, gold and silver jewelry and inlaid marble jewelry boxes.

WHAT TO EAT AND DRINK: Frankly, it is Florence where one goes to eat and drink well. The Tuscan kitchen is considered to be one of the finest in Italy. Dishes are simply flavored, without rich spices and based on hearty, bountiful produce brought in from the hills. Look for **Bistecca alla Fiorentina,** a large T-bone steak grilled over a charcoal fire and brushed with virgin olive oil; **Fettuccine al Burro** are fresh home made noodles served with melted butter and fresh grated Romano cheese; **Spaghetti alla Rustica,** made with a sauce of garlic, oregano, Pecorino cheese and anchovies; **Sigliola al Marsala,** a filet of fresh sole cooked in butter and laced with Marsala wine; **Petit di Pollo alla Bolognese,** are boned chicken breasts topped with a slice of Italian ham, Fontina cheese and baked with thin slices of white truffles; and for dessert, always ask for the Italian **gelato,** ice cream. The Italians are masters at making ice cream.

As to wines: Tuscany is the Chianti capital of the world and you should drink and taste as many different Chianti's as possible. Why? Because they seem to taste better there than in the United States. They travel well but seem to drink better in Florence.

LONDON (England)

WHAT TO SEE: No city in Europe draws more people to its shore than London. Urbane, hospitable and steeped in history, London is truly a sightseer's paradise. There is the House of Parliament, Buckingham Palace, Trafalgar Square, Whitehall Street and the changing of the Guard that are "musts" on your London list. If you participate in Royal Cruise Lines "London Theater Break", then you can enjoy the London theatre and spend two excellent nights at the Park Lane Hotel which overlooks Green Park and Buckingham Palace.

A QUICK GUIDE

Italians are in love with their own romantic and lyrical language and they play a little loose with the titles of restaurants. Here is a one minute guide to Italian restaurants.

RISITORANTE – Expensive, sophisticated and featuring a few Italian dishes with a heavy emphasis on the "international" dishes.

TRATTORIA – Inexpensive, adhering to local foods and wines, featuring modest meals with many of the owner's specialities.

OSTERIA – A country or village Trattoria where simple but very good food is served along with local wines.

TAVOLA CALDA – The Italian version of the fast food snack. Some can be good.

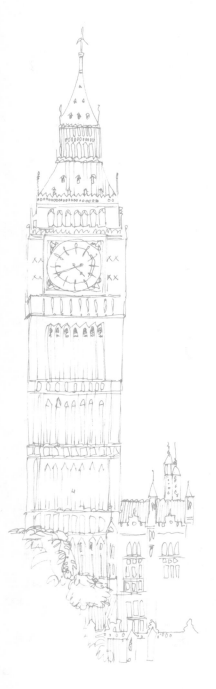

You'll enjoy a full English breakfast every morning and dine at one of the famed restaurants such as Verry's, Louis, Park Lane, Cafe Royal Relais, et cetera.

WHAT TO BUY: Almost anything here is good, especially art objects, antiques, clothes, silver and woolens.

WHAT TO EAT AND DRINK: Long established as the Roast Beef capital of the world, try it with the famed **Yorkshire Pudding;** try **Bubble and Squeak,** thin sliced roast beef sauteed in butter and covered with fried cabbage; **Kippers,** which are the best herrings, split down the back, lightly cured and then smoked on an open fire; **Poor Knights of Windsor,** one of the world's great desserts, consisting of slices of bread soaked in sherry, dipped in milk and egg, sauteed and topped with butter, sherry and sugar sauce.

MALAGA (Spain)

WHAT TO SEE: This old port city and its rich 16th century Cathedral and the current Alcazaba date from the times of the Moors. Leaving Malaga to Granada, you visit the Royal Chapel, the tombs of Ferdinand and Isabella and then drive to the Alhambra and Gardens of Generalife.

WHAT TO BUY: There are dolls, fans, miniature brave bulls, suedes and leather goods, silks and pottery.

WHAT TO EAT AND DRINK: The best seafood on the waterfront east of the pier and Malaga Park is the restaurant **Antonio Martin.** Malaga specialties include **Centollos,** minced spider crabs sauteed in brandy, sherry, tomato sauce, stuffed into the shells and dotted with butter; **Langosta a la Barcelonesa,** chicken and lobster cooked in tomatoes with ground almonds. The best wines are the sherries.

MESSINA (Sicily)

WHAT TO SEE: Sicily is the largest island in the Mediterranean and famous for Mt. Etna, an active volcano and also the largest in Europe. From the ship you can travel through the city and stop outside the Norman-Romanesque Cathedral to view its carved central portal and strange astronomical clock. Go through the coastal hills and citrus groves of the island to the popular resort of Taormina. This town's winding streets have delightful boutiques and shops where souvenirs can be purchased.

WHAT TO BUY: In Messina, Italian fashions are excellent; so is leather, silk, porcelain and ceramics; in Taormina, look for handmade lace dresses, antique bedspreads, wood carvings and ceramics.

WHAT TO EAT AND DRINK: Some specialties you should look for on the menu include **Risotto con Gamberi,** fresh shrimp sauteed in garlic and butter and then a tomato sauce flavored with brandy is added; **Spaghetti alla Carrattiera,** in which the sauce is made from olive oil, tuna fish, and small vegetables that have been soaked in a marinade; **Zuppa di Cozze,** fresh mussel soup slowly simmered to bring out the ocean taste; **Cannoli,** a Sicilian pastry horn filled with sweetened ricotta cheese, candied peel and cocoa. In the wine department try Marsala after dessert and with dinner try the wines from Etna, named Etna.

NAPLES (Italy)

WHAT TO SEE: Founded 600 years before the birth of Christ, Naples is a city to be savored. In Naples travelers will see the Piazza Vittoria, the Via Parthenope, Castell dell'Oro on the romantic fishermen's harbor of Santa Lucia, the Piazza del Plebiscito, the Royal Palace and its adjoining San Carlo Opera House. The National Museum at the Piazzo Museo contains a wealth of finds from Pompeii and Herculaneum. When Vesuvius erupted in 70 A.D., the life of Pompeii was suddenly stopped and today this city is almost in perfect preservation, even though it was unearthed from beneath some 20 feet of volcanic ash and rubble.

WHAT TO BUY: There is beautiful red coral jewelry in many forms and configurations as well as Italian leather goods, silk scarves, neckties, brass and antique items.

WHAT TO EAT AND DRINK: You may not believe this, but pizza is Naples' contribution to the world of Italian cuisine. It is made in the eight inch version and you should try it just for fun. There are some dishes you should taste, among them are **Maccheroni ai Quattero Formaggi,** a special macaroni with four cheeses; **Fritto Misto,** a mixed dish deep fat fried always using the fresh fish caught that day; **Cozze au Gratin,** fresh mussels cooked in white wine, garlic, parsley topped with a creamy rich cheese sauce; **Calzone alla Napolentana,** a huge boat shaped pastry, stuffed with mozzarella, tomato sauce, anchovies and then baked until it puffs up; **Carpaccio,** very thin slices of lean, raw, beef filet pounded as thin as scallopini, dressed with an olive oil, mustard, caper, lemon juice and topped with thin shaved Parmesan cheese. Naples has given us Enrico Caruso and

49

ONE MORE PLEASE!

The cheapest thing you have on a trip is film. That's why it pays to take many shots rather than a few. Beware of the "one shot" pro who never duplicates a picture. He usually is never heard from again. Shoot and shoot again, just to make sure.

Sophia Loren and it has also given us such wines as Lacrima Christi (tears of Christ), grown on the seaward side of Mt. Vesuvius, Ravello wines (Bianco, Rosato and Rosso), Ischia Rossa and Ischia Bianco. These are the wines that match the fine foods of Naples.

NICE (France)

WHAT TO SEE: Said to be the world's most luxurious playground, Nice is the capital of the French good life, nestled in the heart of the great area, Provence.

In the nearby tiny Principality of Monaco, a stop will be made at the Palace of Prince Rainer and Princess Grace. Then it's on to the famous Casino of Monte Carlo, before returning to the ship.

If you would like to visit St. Paul and Cannes you can travel into the foothills of the Alps de Provence on the way to St. Paul. A stone wall encircles this tiny town of cobblestone streets, shops and houses whose weathered red ceramic roofs have baked in the Riviera sun for centuries. You now descend toward the sea to Cannes visiting the chic shops and boutiques. On the way back to the Odyssey, you pass through the towns of Juan-Les-Pins, Antibes and Cagnes-sur-Mer.

WHAT TO BUY: As you would expect from the French, fine perfumes, silk scarves and ties, Limoges porcelain, antiques and original oil and water color paintings are to be had.

WHAT TO EAT AND DRINK: You are in the heart of Provence and their cuisine is sometimes called the "cuisine of the sun." Their cuisine has a hint of garlic, tomatoes, olive oil and herbs de provence, a delightful mixture of appetite stimulators. You must not leave Nice without trying the famous **Bouillabaisse,** made with the real Provencal fish **racasse** and unobtainable in the United States; **Soupe au Pistou,** a vegetable soup to which is added at the last minute a paste made from crushed garlic, basil, cheese and olive oil. **Bagna Cauda,** a warm bath of garlic, anchovies and olive oil into which raw vegetables in season are dipped; **Poulet a la Nicoise,** in which chicken is cooked in lime juice, thyme, salt pork, onions, garlic, tomatoes, white wine and black Nice olives; and **Pissaladiere,** the French version of an onion tart laced as the chef sees fit with anchovies, olives, and loads of onion puree made with bay leaf, onions, thyme.

The wines of Provence match the foods very well. For more than 20 years the wines of Domaine Ott have been my favorate wines of Provence. Look for Domaine Ott's Comtes

de Provence, Rouge, 1978; Clos Mireille, Blancs de Blancs de Provence; a great 1979 and 80 rose, Chateau de Selle and their Bandol Rose, Chateau Marine, 1979 or 1980. Others you might look for are Chateau Minuty and Domaine Tempier.

PALMA DE MALLORCA (Mallorca)

WHAT TO SEE: A favorite Mediterranean resort spa, this port has much to offer the Odyssey passenger. Tour the city of Palma and visit the Cathedral, a city landmark since the 13th century and the hillside Castle of Bellover with its museum surrounded by medieval walls. If you are an adventurous passenger, ride into the hills and northern mountain range where the charming old village of Valldemosa lies just 45 minutes outside the city. Here you will see the Vart Carthusian monastary where during the winter of 1838 Frederick Chopin and French authoress George Sand resided. One optional activity is the medieval dinner of El Comte Mal held in the old estates of the Counts of Mal. A true medieval event complete with authentic games and feats of equestrian dexterity, the banquet features roast suckling pig, Mallorcan sweets and some surprises.

WHAT TO BUY: Be sure to look at the famous man-made pearls, Perles Majorica. There are original oil paintings as well as water colors, handpainted pottery and glassware, easier and lighter to carry are the hand embroidered bridge sets, tablecloths and placemats, all made on the island.

WHAT TO EAT AND DRINK: There are some Catalan specialties such as **Ensaimadas,** a fluffy pastry bread and a local favorite; **Caldera de Peix,** a local fish soup containing many varieties of local fresh caught fish, and one of the best restaurants in Mallorca is **Meson Carlos I** in Palma with a real 16th Century setting. Unless you like sweet liqueurs, stick with the light white and red wines.

LISBON (Portugal)

WHAT TO SEE: One of the largest ports in Europe and the greatest port of Portugal, Lisbon is considered by world travelers as one of Europe's most charming capitals. Built on seven hills, Lisbon lives on two levels with the most picturesque section of the city being Alfama with its narrow cobblestone streets and Moorish arches. In the evening the sad songs about the struggle of life fill the Alfama air along with the staccato rhythms of a too sad guitar.

SPICY ROME

The most lavish users of spices were the Romans. Not only did they use almost all the spices known at that time, they used them in wines, foods, cosmetics, perfumes, oils, funerals, waters, baths, and even rubbed them into their skins. Rome must have smelled nice.

WHAT TO BUY: Portuguese handicrafts, ceramics including vividly decorated roosters, lace, filagree work in both gold and silver wire, baskets and hand woven carpets which combine linen and wool from the village of Arraiolos; leather gloves and suede, cork objects, hand carvings and Madeira embroidery and applique or fashioned into tablecloths, placemats and cocktail napkins.

WHAT TO EAT AND DRINK: Portuguese cuisine is peasant cuisine, because they make use of local products and don't go about trying to import food stuffs and ingredients. That means the best are lobsters, suckling pigs, grilled fish and fresh vegetables. They are also excellent with game. Dishes you should try if you see them on the menu include **Ameijoas a Bulhao Pato,** which are clams cooked with garlic and coriander; **Frango no espeto a moda de Minho,** a real barnyard chicken brushed with olive oil, chili sauce and spit roasted over hardwood; **Bacalhau,** the excellent Portuguese salt cod of which it is said that there are 365 ways to cook it, one for every day of the year; **Cozido a Portugusea,** a delicious stew of various meats always including beef, chicken and sausage with rice cooked in stock and vegetables; **Feijao guisado,** a famous kidney bean stew with bacon and tomato sauce; **Caldo verda,** a cabbage soup eaten for both lunch and dinner with dark corn bread and Leitao assado, a spit roasted suckling pig.

Portuguese wines are very good. Try the Vinho Verde wine from Minho, the best coming from Moncao and the Dao wines both in red with white. And by all means have a glass of tawny port or Vintage port for dessert. It is a must.

VENICE (Italy)

WHAT TO SEE: Venice consists of 117 islands, 150 canals, 400 bridges and hundreds of gondolas to whisk you around at any time of day or night. The best way to tour Venice is by foot starting at St. Mark's Square, where you can always sip a Campari and soda or Capuccino coffee, watch the people and the hundreds of pigeons go by. As you walk around Venice you will be impressed by this silent city surrounded by water. You can gamble at the famed Lido, tour the famous Grand Canal, visit the old Clock Tower and Bell Tower in St. Mark's Square, visit San Vio to see handmade glass being blown and join a flotilla of gondolas and listen to the magic of Italian music as you float and take in the mystery that is Venice.

WHAT TO BUY: Leather, silks and Venetian glass.

WHAT TO EAT AND DRINK: Venetians are said to have invented the fork and table napkin while others were still eating with their fingers. Try **Pate di Fegato alla Veneziana,** a mixture of equal parts of calf's liver and butter, laced with brandy; **Risi e Bisi,** a Venetian invention of peas, olive oil, bacon, onions, stock and Parmesan cheese; **Torresani,** small semi-domesticated pigeons which are spit roasted over grape stakes. There are some 60 different wines to choose from, but you should try Valpolicella, Bardolino and Soave.

HIGHLIGHTS FROM THE EASTERN MEDITERRANEAN AND GREEK ISLES

CAIRO (Egypt)

WHAT TO SEE: The Odyssey's full-day call in Egypt will provide vacationers with memories that will last a lifetime. The ship docks early morning at Alexandria. From here, passengers will have the opportunity to experience the oriental capital city of Cairo just before journeying across the sandy Sahara desert. Excursionists will pass through suburban Heliopolis enroute to Cairo and its Egyptian Museum to view treasures dating back to Pharonic times, including the dazzling collection of gold, jewelry and furnishings from the tomb of King Tutankhamon, a collection which far surpasses the treasures that recently toured the United States. Then they will cross the Nile to Giza, on the periphery of the West Desert. Here, monuments stand denoting ancient man's artistry and engineering: The Great Pyramid of Cheops (first and oldest of the Seven Wonders of the World), the Pyramids of Chefren and Mykerinos and the legendary Sphinx. Camel rides, sand carts or horses will be available, as well as a visit of the interior chambers of one of the pyramids. Leaving these marvels of antiquity, passengers return to Cairo to visit the Mosque of Mohammed Ali and Citadel with its view westward across Cairo to the pyramids.

WHAT TO BUY: The best buys are Egyptian brass and silver trays and jewelry, leather bags, hassocks, Egyptian crafts and antiques.

WHAT TO EAT AND DRINK: Egyptian food falls into the Middle Eastern school of cookery. The quality of the food is excellent. Some dishes to try include **Fattah,** a creamy baked combination of rice, Arab bread, chopped chicken and yogurt; **Dolma,** a variety of lamb and rice stuffed vegetables of

LITTLE FOOLER

The Egyptian King kept yelling "Fool, Fool." He wasn't scolding someone; he was asking for:

1. Beans
2. Dates
3. Onions
4. Spices

Give up?

1. Beans, because they were an Egyptian staple

53

grape leaves and the local caviar, **Bathrikh,** is very good. Egyptian wines are getting better and better and the local beer, Stella, is good.

ATHENS (Greece)

WHAT TO SEE: This is a world famous jet set resort city and ancient Greek capital. Athens gained her reputation during the 5th Century B.C., the "golden age" and its rich monuments to this period, such as the Acropolis (sacred hill), overlooking the city; Hill of Philopappou, even higher than the Acropolis; Temple of Hephaisteion; the Agora, a gathering place for the Athenians for more than 1,000 years; Portico of the Giants; the foundations of the Council House and the Odeon.

WHAT TO BUY: The Athens flea market is a must for shopping addicts for here are authentic antiques, religious icons, designer fashions and handmade jewelry from the boutiques along the streets of Panepistimiou and Voukourestiou.

WHAT TO EAT AND DRINK: Besides the excellent Greek foods and wines served aboard the Odyssey, you might like to visit the great Greek tavernas that abound in Athens to sample **Taramasalata,** a wonderful fish roe appetizer made with lemon juice, olive oil and soaked breadcrumbs; **Faki,** lentil soup with onion, garlic, bay leaves, olive oil and vinegar; **Sofrito,** slices of steak stewed in vinegar and water with garlic until a thick sauce emerges and **Psari Plaki,** fish baked with a thick sauce of onions, garlic, tomato, parsley and wine. Wine names to remember are Demestica, Mavroudi and Hymettus. If in doubt, ask the Odyssey wine stewards. They will know.

CORFU (Greece)

WHAT TO SEE: Considered the most beautiful of the Ionian Islands, Corfu is 40 miles long and 20 miles wide, with a population of 150,000. Investigate the old town from the arcaded Spianada (esplanade) to the streets behind. Visit the 16th century Cathedral dedicated to the island's patron saint, Spyridion. Walk or take a horse and buggy along the coastal area called Garitsa with a magnificent view of the crests crowned by a Venetian fortress. To see rural Corfu,

drive through the rolling hills and olive groves to the ornate Achilleion Palace, former villa of Empress Elizabeth of Austria which is now a museum by day and a casino by night.

WHAT TO BUY: Jewelry, worry beads, Greek shoulder bags, olive wood bowls, hand knit sweaters, fur rugs and copies of ancient artists are some of the gifts you can bring back.

WHAT TO EAT AND DRINK: For food see above. For drink, try and bring back some kumquat liqueur, one of the rarest of liqueurs.

HAIFA AND THE HOLY LANDS

WHAT TO SEE: Israel's port city of Haifa brings passengers to another historic highlight: the Holy Lands. A day and a half visit and comprehensive optional tours insure that Odyssey passengers will have ample opportunity to experience the full cultural significance of this region. The Jerusalem and Bethlehem tour departs from Haifa for a drive along the coast and eastward up into the hills of Judea. Passing through New Jerusalem past the Knesset, Israel's Parliament, excursionists will go on to the little village of Bethlehem, the site of Rachel's tomb and birthplace of King David and Jesus. Then there will be a visit to the Basilica of the Nativity and shopping time around Manger Square. In Jerusalem passengers may also visit the Mount of Olives, view the Valley of Kidron, the famous Western Wall (formerly the "Wailing Wall") and walk to the Church of the Holy Sepulchre.

Nazareth and the Sea of Galilee are also destinations available to Odyssey passengers taking them north and eastward into fertile Galilee. A beautiful part of Israel, this was the area of Jesus' "hidden years". After a visit to Nazareth, with its Well of Mary and Church of the Annunciation, the tour will continue on into Galilee to the Biblical villages of Cana (site of the first miracle of Jesus), Tabgah (place of the multiplication of the loaves and fishes), Magdala and Capernaum, with its ancient Jewish Synagogue on the shore of the Sea of Galilee.

WHAT TO BUY: Olive wood, silver and gold jewelry, ceramics, Israeli textiles and fashions, handblown glass and religious artifacts.

BIG DEALER

Every great man or women has had a variety of jobs. One of the greatest leaders of the world was once a spice dealer. He was:

a. Jesus Christ
b. Mohammed
c. Martin Luther
d. Columbus

b. He once worked as a tradesman selling spices.

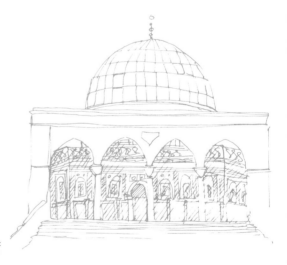

55

THE BEST SHOW IN THE WORLD

Your eye can fool you when you take pictures. It is the camera eye that takes just what it shows you. Too many people think that what they see through their eyes is what the camera will show. Wrong! For the best pictures in the world, forget what your eyes show you and stick with what you see through the lens.

WHAT TO EAT AND DRINK: If at all possible try **Schav,** an ice cold sorrel soup garnished with sliced hard boiled eggs and sour cream; **Gikochteh Hindel,** chicken stewed in onions and paprika; **Tzimmes,** slow cooked casserole of brisket sweetened with carrots, syrup, prunes, topped with potatoes and dumplings, and for dessert **Hamantaschen,** three cornered cakes stuffed with wine, walnuts, poppy seeds, apple and apricot mixture.

Israeli wines to look for on wine lists include Chateau Windsor (red), Mont Rouge (red), Carmel (white), Chateau Montague (white). Look for a sparkling wine named President. It is good.

ISTANBUL (Turkey)

WHAT TO SEE: Once the seat of the powerful Ottoman Empire, Istanbul (when I was a kid it was called Constantinople) is the largest city and port in the Turkish Republic. This city is a perfect setting for an Orson Welles thriller. The old walled city is located on the European side of the Bosphorus Strait, which connects the Sea of Marmara to the Black Sea. At the north end of this city of seven hills is a narrow inlet, the Golden Horn, which also forms part of the Istanbul Harbor. Here is an opportunity to cross the Golden Horn to tour the oldest quarter of the city, Constantinople, rebuilt after the ancient wars by Emperor Constantine in the 4th Century. Santa Sophia, the architectural miracle of the 6th Century A.D. and the "soul" of East Roman or Byzantine Empire, is still there, and today is a museum.

WHAT TO BUY: A shopper's paradise is the Grand Covered Bazaar where samovars (Russian urns), copperware, old glassware, embroideries, onyx and alabaster Turkish Pipes and Turkish confections are for sale.

WHAT TO EAT AND DRINK: Turkish food is excellent. Their version of **Rice Pilaff** contains rice cooked with pine nuts, currants, and aromatic spices usually served with chicken or lamb; **Borek,** small pastry envelopes filled with a meat, vegetable or cheese mixture, served as a main course and **Cerkez Tavugu,** known as "Circassian chicken", is shredded chicken in a pink cold sauce of walnuts, garlic, bread-crumbs, paprika and chicken stock. Turkish wines can be very good. Buzbag, Doluca and Trakya are what to look for.

KUSADASI AND IZMIR (Turkey)

WHAT TO SEE: From either of these port cities, passengers can visit the ancient first century ruins of Biblical Ephesus, once famous in antiquity for the Temple of Diana, one of the seven wonders of the ancient world and later the home of St. John. During the reign of the Roman Empire, Ephesus became the greatest city in Asia Minor. Ephesus's archeological site is entered through the Magnesia Gate, where a walk down its majestic marble street takes a visitor past extensive excavations of this once important city.

WHAT TO BUY: You will find brass and copper artifacts, Turkish slippers and robes. Oriental carpets including Persian and Turkish rugs, pottery, Meerschaum pipes and water pipes can also be purchased.

WHAT TO EAT AND DRINK: Save your appetites for Istanbul.

MYKONOS (Greece)

WHAT TO SEE: This tiny island located in the middle of the Aegean Sea between Turkey and Greece, has come into international popularity in recent years with travellers for its simplicity and old world charm. Overlooking the seaport town and the inviting blue water are lovely white villas stretched along the roadside. There are the famous windmills which have become the island's trademark.

WHAT TO BUY: A stroll past the waterfront shops and boutiques offers a visitor the opportunity to purchase gold and silver jewelry, high fashions, handknit sweaters, handwoven fabrics, crocheted shawls, dresses and handbags, and worry beads.

WHAT TO EAT: If you are not going back to the ship to have supper, here are a few dinner suggestions: **Exokhiko,** small packages of flaky filo pastry filled with a lamb chop, peas, potatoes, tomatoes, Kaseri cheese, parsley and baked in the oven; **Domates Yemistes,** tomatoes stuffed with ground veal, onions, mint, parsley, rice, topped with fresh breadcrumbs and baked or perhaps a light dessert with

57

coffee, such as **Baklavas,** a light thin flaky pastry made from filo and stuffed with almonds, walnuts, sugar, cinnamon, and baked in the oven and then topped with hot syrup and served cold.

RHODES (Greek Isles)

WHAT TO SEE: World-famous for its lovely flower-filled landscape of gentle, rolling hills, Rhodes' history dates back to mythological times when sun-blessed Rhodes was the island of the god Apollo. Its actual history dates back to the 15th Century B.C., when its earliest visitors, the Mycenaeans, first arrived. Subsequently the island went through Roman, Gothic, English, Turkish and Italian occupation finally reverting back to Greece in 1945. When visitors arrive outside the walled city, they may take a walk through the Porte d'Amboise and then to the Castle of the Knights (today known as the Knights of Malta). Strolling down the Street of the Knights takes one past Renaissance Inns of the Knights to the former Hospital of the Order, now an archeological museum which houses the classical sculpture of Aphrodite. A more extended tour takes passengers from shipside to the picturesque village of Lindos dotted with ruins of ancient temples, a medieval palace, the Byzantine Church of St. John and the famous Temple of Athena Linda.

WHAT TO BUY: Shopping specials include brass and copper souvenirs, hand painted ceramics and hand made jewelry.

WHAT TO EAT AND DRINK: Try the Greek foods mentioned above and on the previous page.

CRETE (Heraklion, Greece)

WHAT TO SEE: Passing from the port through provencial Heraklion, drive into the countryside to nearby Knossos where local guides direct you through the labyrinthian Palace of King Minos. Good walking shoes and comfortable clothes are in order for this — and every — excursion! The Heraklion Museum will also be visited and is worth every effort (in spite of resounding accoustics).

It is a 10 to 15 minute walk from the pier to the "main street" and the Venetian Morosini Fountain with its surrounding shops and book stores. Other shops are found near the Museum. For swimming the E.O.T. Beach is best: a taxi ride out and the taxi should be asked to wait to bring you back.

HIGHLIGHTS FROM THE
CARIBBEAN / SOUTH AMERICA / MEXICAN RIVIERA

ACAPULCO (Mexico)

WHAT TO SEE: Someone once wrote that this city is the international seaside-cabana-bikini-hotel-swimming-pool-jet-set resort. It is blessed with eternal sunshine, no neckties, siestas and whatever you like anytime of the year. During the day you can tour the commercial area of this village and see the young men who defy death diving 136 feet into the Pacific Ocean below with its sinister and swirling waters. Cruisers can adventure into Acapulco's nightlife which is an exciting combination of food, fun and festivities. The Odyssey will be your hotel for your overnight stay here.

WHAT TO BUY: The "made in Acapulco" items include baskets, Mexican silver, copper, tin, leather goods, tortoise and bone souvenirs, handwoven serapes, rugs and pottery.

WHAT TO EAT AND DRINK: Acapulco doesn't have a special cuisine of its own but it is Latin in character. Some dishes to look for include **Chicken or Turkey Mole,** a specialty of Mexico made with Mole sauce, which takes 3 days to make; **Fipian Chicken,** cooked with sesame seed and pumpkin seed sauce and **Chiles en Nogado,** one of the best stuffed pepper dishes with ground pork, onions, almonds topped with a walnut, cheese and spice sauce. Look for wines from Baja or California. Beer, too, is excellent; my favorite is Dos Equis or Superior.

ARUBA (Netherlands Antilles)

WHAT TO SEE: Well known for its magnificent white, sandy beaches and giant boulders randomly strewn about the island, Aruba is the most westerly of the leeward Netherland Antilles. Cruisers may venture on the island through the countryside to see the Natural Bridge and the strange rock formation garden of Casibari, with its natural plantation of

RELAX

If there is one secret to cruise enjoyment it is summed up in a single word — relax. Let the worries and cares you left behind stay there. Don't worry about what you will do or who you will meet, or what you will say. Remember, everyone is in the same boat.

Aruban "dividivi" trees. Visit St. Anne's Church with its hand carved oak altar and drive through Noord to Aruba's famed Palm Beach.

WHAT TO BUY: Best buys are Swiss watches, English bone China, European silver and pewter, British woolens and Haitian wood carvings.

WHAT TO EAT AND DRINK: Best home-devised dishes are **Stoba,** a lamb or goat stew and **Sopito,** a fish chowder that owes its special flavor to coconut milk. Favorite Aruban snacks are **Avacas,** a leaf-wrapped meat roll; **Pastechi,** a meat-stuffed turnover and **Cala,** bean fritters. Most exotic eating is Indonesian **Rijsttafel,** which offers as many as 25 different dishes to accompany your rice. Stay with the Spanish red and white wines.

BARBADOS

WHAT TO SEE: Named Los Barbados — the bearded ones — for the banyan trees with their shaggy, exposed roots, this "Little England" offers Odyssey cruisers a view of private estates and such luxury hotels as Sandy Lane.

On the eastern side of the island, you can visit St. John's Church and Sam Lord's Castle, now a hotel, to get a sense of the lifestyle such island pirates as Lord became accustomed to. The capital city of Bridgetown is a must for sightseers and shoppers and is just a mile from the ship. Here shopping is available in Trafalgar Square on Broad Street.

WHAT TO BUY: Local handmade straw goods, shells and shell art, tortoise shell and coconut jewelry, wood bowls and masks and imported European duty free gifts.

WHAT TO EAT AND DRINK: The national dish of the "Bajans" is the flying fish and oddly enough the perfect visitor food. Other specialties include **Oursin,** sea urchins that are minced, devilled and coated with bread crumbs; **Souse,** a melange of pig pickled with onion, cucumber and pepper; **Coo Coo,** a cake made from cornmeal and okra; **Creole Pepperpot** is just about the same as the one served in St. Barts, and try a nonalcoholic drink made from bark, sugar and spices called **Mauby,** a drink that is served in many Bajans' homes. And don't forget the Barbados rum, said to be the smoothest, richest and best in the world.

CARACAS (Venezuela)

WHAT TO SEE: This is a city of contrasts with its 20th Century architecture and quaint colonial homes. Twenty-five years ago cattle were being driven down dirt roads on the outskirts of the town; today there are freeways and high rises.

Historic landmarks are abundant throughout the city and include the National Pantheon, where the remains of Liberator Simon Bolivar and other national heroes rest, the Old El Silencio quarter and Miraflores Palace. Of special historical interest are visits to the Casa Natal where Bolivar was born, and the Caracas Mansion, now the Colonial Museum.

WHAT TO BUY: Shops carry a variety of wood handicrafts, straw bags, papier mache devil masks, woven hammocks, rag dolls and some of the South American low lustre cochano 18K gold jewelry.

WHAT TO EAT AND DRINK: Be prepared to pay $25 to $30 per person for such specialties as **Tequenos,** a popular hors d'oeuvres of dough wrapped around a finger of white cheese and fried crisp; **Pabellon Criollo,** shredded meat, fried plantains and black beans on rice; **Cazon,** ground shark meat; **Hallacas,** banana leaves stuffed with a mixture of cornmeal, beef, pork, ham, pepper, onions and olives and **Medallon de lomito al Oporto,** steak cooked in port wine. Try the locally made Sangrias for a change of drink.

CARTAGENA (Colombia)

WHAT TO SEE: This South American colonial port, with its narrow Boca Chica fort lined entrance, gives a visitor a sense of the flavor of Colombia's centuries old domination of the New World. All the gold and treasures from other 16th century Spanish colonies were once held in the fort of San Felipe for shipment to Spain. This made the city a prime target for pirate attacks for some 200 years. Forts, plus a ring of fortified wall seven miles long, 40 feet high and 55 feet thick were built over a period of some 230 years to completely encircle the city. Other attractions include a trip to La Popa, the highest point in the city, founded by the Augustine Fathers in 1607, whose successors still reside there.

WHAT TO BUY: Emeralds (95% of the world's emeralds are mined in Colombia), macrame, shawls, purses, silver and gold jewelry, leather goods and Colombian coffee.

CAMERA CARE

While any cruise is a photographer's paradise, it is not always paradise for your equipment. Color film is sensitive to heat, so when not taking pictures, protect your camera from the sun. Salt air is corrosive, so wipe the outside periodically with a cloth. If you don't have a lens cleaner, breathe gently on the filter before wiping it with a soft, dust-free cloth or lens tissue.

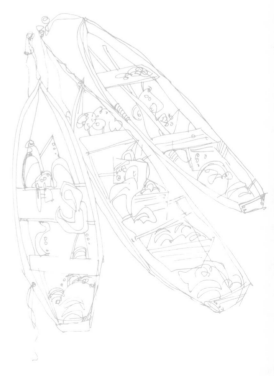

QUICK DELIVERY

On St. Thomas, USVI, liquor is such a popular item that some of the more aggressive stores will come aboard, take your orders, and deliver the five pack in bond before you have a chance to say yes or no.

PANAMA CITY (Republic of Panama)

WHAT TO SEE: The progress of this republic can be seen in the mingling of balcony lined old buildings and the high-rise structures. You can visit the Church of the Golden Altar, French Plaza, the flat arch of Santo Domingo and the statue of explorer Vasco Numez de Balboa. Early Panama history can be seen in the ruins of Old Panama, the first city founded in 1519, later sacked and razed by the pirate Henry Morgan in 1671.

WHAT TO BUY: Panama hats, of course, here called "montuno", and duty free items such as imported china, crystal, linens, locally made silver and gold jewelry.

WHAT TO EAT & DRINK: Panama food is international, a mixture of French, Spanish and American Cuisines. Some is a blend between the Creole cuisine of Haiti and New Orleans. Two specialties include **Sanchoo,** a meat and chicken stew mixed with a variety of vegetables and **Sarima Olas,** special small pies filled with meat, chicken or cheese. Rice is eaten at least twice a day along with a variety of beans. Try the local beer with this food.

ST. LUCIA (British Commonwealth)

WHAT TO SEE: Still considered as the "unspoiled" island surviving in the Caribbean today, St. Lucia has some of the most magnificent shoreline in the world. Odyssey cruisers can see this beautiful island by the "Queen's Route" tour, because Queen Elizabeth traveled this itinerary when she visited here in 1966.

An Odyssey's St. Lucia tour shows off the breathtaking beauty and dramatic terrain of this West Indies island, stopping at the sulphur springs, known locally as the "drive-in volcano" and viewing the Grand Piton and Petit Piton, the lava plugs of now extinct volcanos.

WHAT TO BUY: There are many original St. Lucian items such as handprinted batik, straw bags, placemats and trivets, sculpture and The Bagshaws' handscreened prints of dresses, placemats, scarves and fabrics.

WHAT TO EAT AND DRINK: The island specialties are very good. Try **Callaloo soup,** which contains dasheen leaves, crabs, okras, onions, chives, garlic, pork and salt beef; **Crab-In-The-Back** are crab backs stuffed with spiced crab and lobster meat and **Banana Bread** is just what it sounds like. Wines are French and can be expensive.

ST. MAARTEN/ST. MARTIN (Dutch Netherland Antilles)

WHAT TO SEE: When Columbus landed here in 1493, this island was owned by the natives. Today, the island is the smallest piece of land anywhere in the world shared by two sovereign powers, France and Holland. The Dutch half, Saint Maarten, is 17 square miles, while the French half, St. Martin, is 20 square miles.

This small island, indented by beautiful bays (there must be more than 100) is hilly in the center and slopes toward the seashore forming picturesque beaches (there are 36 beaches to choose from); the vegetation is tropical and both the hills and flatlands are lush and green.

WHAT TO BUY: Shopping in Philipsburg is duty free since there are no local taxes. Dutch silver, cameras, Delft china, perfumes, and Swiss watches are on sale in the town's small shops and boutiques.

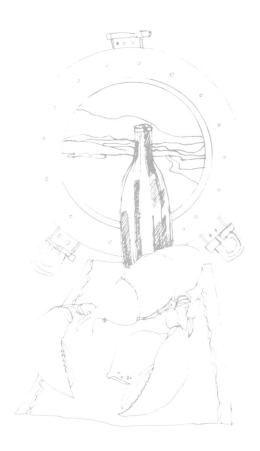

WHAT TO EAT AND DRINK: If you enjoy French cuisine, this is a good place to sample both the classic version as well as the Creole version. Here again it is **Lobster** in any shape or form plus fresh **Fish** of all kinds; **Curried Conch** and **Chicken Colombos,** for curry lovers and a savory fish stew called **Blaff.** French wines are available and so is Dutch beer.

ST. THOMAS (Virgin Islands, United States)

WHAT TO SEE: Our old friend Columbus discovered these islands on his second voyage in 1493 and thanks to him, you and I can enjoy some of the most beautiful islands in the world. The Virgin Islands, the nearest things to a home port for the likes of Captain Kidd, Blackbeard and Sir Francis Drake are full of dramatic peaks and spectacular jagged bays. Of course, no visitor to St. Thomas will want to miss the old Danish warehouse which houses some of the best and most attractive shopping districts on the island. You might like to take a tour to Coral World, a spectacular underwater ob-

FAST SHIP

The average time for a ship to pass through the Canal waters is 8 hours. The fastest transit was 4 hours and 38 minutes, set by the USS Manley.

servatory which looks out onto a lighted ocean floor filled with rare and beautiful tropical fish, coral formations, and sea life.

WHAT TO BUY: There is a special $600 duty free exemption on items purchased in St. Thomas. There are many excellent wines and liqueurs which you can purchase at liberal discounts as well as fashions, watches, cameras and jewelry.

WHAT TO EAT AND DRINK: While the cuisine is limited, it is good. Try any of the **Fish Soups** since they are made daily from fresh fish; **Turtle Steaks** fixed in a variety of ways and always fresh; **Grundy,** herring balls, and **Soursop,** a local fruit made into ice cream. As for wine, ask for the "vins du pays" of the Virgin Islands, and you will be surprised.

SAN BLAS ISLANDS (Panama)

WHAT TO SEE: Situated along the western shores of the Caribbean, all of the approximately 500 islands on the chain belong to the Cuna Indians. Their civilization is best known for their colorful "molas". These bright rectangles of layered cloth, appliqued and reverse appliqued with geometric designs or representations of mythological or real flora and fauna, can be found in shops from Hong Kong to New York. Odyssey passengers will have an opportunity to visit the island and tour the Cuna dwellings to see their way of life.

WHAT TO BUY: Wood carvings, bead bracelets, imolas and gourd rattles.

WHAT TO EAT AND DRINK: Enjoy lunch aboard ship.

SAN JUAN (Puerto Rico)

WHAT TO SEE: Old San Juan is literally across the street from where the Odyssey is docked and it is just a short walk to this historic section. Make sure you visit the 16th century El Morro, the giant fortress at the end of seven square block Old San Juan. Walk through the Plaza de Armas where small shops and galleries line the Calle Fortaleza, Calle San Francisco and Calle Cristo. Flower filled balconies and intimate

interior patios are a part of the Spanish influence in the Colonial Old Town. Some historic landmarks to see are the San Jose Church, the Dominican Convent and the Cathedral.

WHAT TO BUY: Local souvenirs are santos, the traditional small religious figures carved from wood; lace, handwoven fabrics, papier mache products, various objects carved from horn and of course, rum, for Puerto Rico is the world's largest producer. Being a U. S. territory, there is no duty on purchases made in San Juan.

WHAT TO EAT AND DRINK: Here are some San Juan specialties you should try: **Arroz Con Pollo,** chicken cooked in stock and spices and served with rice; **Tostones,** deep fried plantain slices, served as a side dish; **Pasteles,** spicy meat patties wrapped in plantain flour dough and baked in plantain leaves; **Jueyes,** land crabs, deviled and served in their shells and **Yechon Asado,** roast suckling pig. Wines are expensive here so I suggest the special island brewed India beer.

HIGHLIGHTS OF SCANDINAVIA / BALTIC SEA

BERGEN (Norway)

WHAT TO SEE: The Odyssey arrives at Bergen, Norway, its northernmost port of call, after an early morning passage through four beautiful fjords: Byfjord, Raunefjord, Korsfjord and Bjornafjord. The charm of this 900 year old city is almost indefinable with its cobbled streets, medieval houses, the age old fish market and the famous warehouses of the Hanseatic period.

WHAT TO BUY: Shopping, of course, is a must and some of the old shops and boutiques afford such treasures as exquisite Norwegian crystal, Norwegian enamelware, pewter, sweaters, and handcrafted items.

WHAT TO EAT AND DRINK: If you have a palate that likes something different, try **Dyrestk,** roast venison served with goat's cheese and red currant jelly, **Lapskaus,** a thick soup of chopped pork and vegetables; **Rekesaus,** shrimp in a cream, milk, butter and lemon juice sauce flavored with fresh dill and **Blotkake,** a cake sponge filled with cream, fresh fruit and covered with thick cream. To drink with this food, try Champagne or any sparkling wine.

COPENHAGEN (Denmark)

WHAT TO SEE: Copenhagen is truly a fairytale city famous for fun, food and the friendly Danes. Founded more than 800 years ago, Copenhagen offers a storybook-like appearance with its old winding streets, open squares, meandering canals, well preserved buildings, and delightful shops and restaurants.

WHAT TO BUY: The Stroeget, the pedestrian shopping street, is one of the greatest shopping experiences in Scandanavia. Special items to look for are Georg Jensen designs, Danish and Greenland furs and silver, Royal Copenhagen, Bing and Grondahl procelain, crystalware, knitwear, linen and antiques.

WHAT TO EAT AND DRINK: There are two words for Danish cuisine: simple and straightforward. And they use a minimum of sauces and disguises. There is one restaurant here that boasts 200 different kinds of Danish "buttered bread" (Smorgasbord) or open faced sandwiches. Dishes you should look for include **Gravlaks,** raw salmon filets marinated in spices, cognac and dill for several days; **Frikadeller,** a typical Danish dish made from mixtures of finely ground beef, or ve'al or pork, formed into balls, fried in butter and served hot or cold. Best drinks are beer and Akvavit, a Swedish powerhouse.

HENSINKI (Finland)

WHAT TO SEE: The contemporary effect of Helsinki is balanced with the surrounding untouched scenery and townscapes. Cruise vacationers may elect to take a city tour passing Senate Square, the old administrative center of Helsinki, the colorful market square, the Parliament Building, Jan Sibelius monument and on to Tapiola, a city known for its distinctive architecture.

WHAT TO BUY: A shopping spree to any one of a dozen boutiques, marketplaces and market halls will provide visitors with a vast selection of Finnish goods such as pottery, "Ryijy" rugs, wood carvings, articles made of woven birch bark, reeds or wicker, Finnish jewelry and furs.

WHAT TO EAT AND DRINK: You can meet and eat a combination of foods in Helsinki. For strictly Finnish food try **Kala-**

kukko, a pork and herring pie; **Makkara** is composed of un-cooked sausages, salami, luncheon meats and served with a brown sauce; **Oopperavoileipa,** an open sandwich with a thick slice of ham topped with fried eggs and **Kiisseli,** the perfect dessert soup made with berries, sugar and thick-ened with potato flour and served cold. The Finns drink but-termilk with their foods and sometimes beer.

LENINGRAD (Russia)

WHAT TO SEE: Leningrad is often described as one of the most beautiful cities in the world. Built by Czar Peter the Great in the 18th Century as a tribute to Western European art and architecture, Leningrad is truly majestic with its straight wide streets and avenues colored with beautiful parks and gardens. Venetian-like waterways run through this city of incredible history and culture. Passengers may highlight their full day visit with a tour of the Winter Palace, the famed Hermitage, which houses an art collection num-bering over 3 million pieces by the great masters including Rembrandt, Renoir, Van Gogh, da Vinci, and Matisse to name a few.

WHAT TO BUY: Most of your shopping will be done at the GUM, the government owned department store. Good buys include multicolored lacquer works in big cannisters and small bowls; tea cozies are nice, enameled thimbles, cup and tea glass holders, and carved ivory.

WHAT TO EAT AND DRINK: Here are some dishes that will give you a sample of Russian cooking. **Solyanka** is a stur-geon soup with cabbage, tomatoes, lemons, olives and capers; **Pojarsky,** cutlets made from chicken, coated with bread crumbs and sauteed; **Lulu Kabobs,** ground lamb patties broiled on skewers; **Lobio,** a dish composed of white beans with ground walnuts and for a different treat try **Buzhenina,** a large ham baked in beer. Drink wines from Georgia; try the white Napureouli and Tsinandali, the red Mukuzani, and Mzvane or Mtzvane.

STOCKHOLM (Sweden)

WHAT TO SEE: Stockholm is a city situated on 14 individual islands separated by varied waterways and bays. Here, ul-tramodern city buildings are subtly blended into the 13th

A WORD TO THE WISE

Everyone on a cruise likes to spend some time in the sun. Did you know that the best hours for tanning are the sunlight hours before 10:00 a.m. and after 2:00 p.m. Be-tween those two times, the sun is the strongest and you are subject to overexposure.

Century structures and cobblestone alleyways of Gamla Stan, the Old Town, taking visitors back to medieval times. The Royal Palace is still the home of the King of Sweden, and the daily changing of the Royal Guard is a colorful, memorable sight.

WHAT TO BUY: Swedish specialties including crystal, cutlery, tableware, textiles and furs.

WHAT TO EAT AND DRINK: Of course there is Smorgasbord, which is still the greatest bargain going today. And the Swedish people don't turn their heads no matter how many times you go back to the table.

The native cuisine has several exclusive specialties; **Gravlax,** a mild cured salmon sliced paper thin usually served as a first course; **Bruna Bonor,** brown beans mixed with slivers of salt pork in a very sweet/sour sauce; **Glasmastarsill,** herring mixed with vinegar, carrots, onions and horseradish; **Kalvfrikasse,** a dish of boiled veal with a dill, caper sauce thickened with egg yolks, and **Risgrynsgrot,** a special rice porridge served with cinnamon and sugar which makes an excellent dessert.

The friendly Cuna's of Panama

Fish

I'LL TAKE TWO

Lobster is one of the great taste treats. Because there are so few and they are so much in demand, they will always be expensive. However, the lobster is a hardy creature. It hasn't changed in:

a. 100,000 years
b. 1,000,000 years
c. 10,000,000 years
d. 100,000,000 years

d. The lobster is one of natures most successful competitors.

Fish are one of those "iffy" dishes; the "iffy" being whether or not the fish is fresh or frozen. I personally serve my guests fresh fish because the taste is better and the texture is better. A few months ago my daughter and I sampled a Sunday brunch. One of the offerings was a seafood crepe. The crepe and the sauce were outstanding but the fish inside the crepe was dry and unacceptable. The fish had been frozen and left in the blazer pan too long so it became tough and inedible.

Man has been eating fish since prehistory. The first fishermen captured fish with their bare hands, a practice Californians still use today when the Grunion swim onto the beaches to spawn. By the Middle Ages, fleets of ships were selling millions of pounds of fish to many nations. Today because of overfishing and pollution, fishermen have to go farther and farther out to sea to catch fish.

Aboard the Odyssey only the freshest fish is served prompting many cruisers to remark how outstanding the fish is cooked and served.

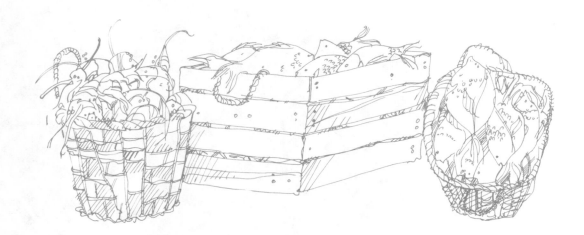

Psaria Plaki

One of the best ways to serve any fish is to bake it. That's because you can control the final product better than if you pan fry it and baking allows you to add a few more ingredients to bring out the taste.

1/2 cup olive oil
8 large onions, sliced
2 cloves garlic, minced
2 Tbs. butter
6 slices sea bass or similar fish steaks
2 tsps. salt
1 tsp. pepper, fresh ground
6 tomatoes, sliced
2 lemons, sliced
1/4 cup dry white wine

Heat the oil in a large saucepan and cook the onions and garlic until golden brown. Melt the butter in a large baking dish and arrange the fish in it so there is space between each slice. Put a tomato slice on each fish slice and top with a lemon slice. Spread rest of tomato and lemon slices around the fish and add the onions and garlic. Add wine and bake at 375 degrees for 30 minutes. To serve, spoon equal portions of the sauce over each fish slice. Serves 6.

OYSTERS, ANYONE?

Oysters Rockefeller, Oysters Ellis, Oysters Bienville, Oysters Thermidor, oysters any way is all right with me. And with a dry white wine they are even better. However, experts can tell the age of an oyster by:

a. Measuring its diameter
b. Weighing them individually
c. Counting the ridges on the outside of the shell
d. Weighing a dozen at a time

c. Determining an oysters age is like counting the rings of a tree.

Apetziota

LUCKY LOBSTERS

Canadian government biologists claim that it makes no difference how you cook a lobster because:

1. Their hard shells protect them from pain.
2. Their bodies adapt quickly to sudden temperature changes.
3. They are deaf to temperature changes.
4. They have no nervous system.

Give up?

4. They have no nervous system and cannot feel anything.

When a chef finds several recipes that are excellent or even exceptional, he refines them to suit his guests' tastes. This has always been a rule with the Odyssey chefs.

1 lb. filets of red snapper, pompano, turbot or sea bass
1/2 tsp. salt
Juice of one large lemon
2 cloves garlic, minced
2 Tbs. minced parsley
2 tomatoes, seeded and chopped fine
1/2 cup olive oil

Spread the filets skin side down on a baking pan. Sprinkle with the salt and lemon juice and let marinate for 30 minutes. Combine the remaining ingredients and evenly spread them over the fish. Preheat the oven to 450 degrees. Place the fish in the oven and lower the temperature to 350 and bake 20-25 minutes or until the fish flakes easily with the fork. Serves 4.

Filet of Sole Louisiana

It avoids combat, preferring to burrow itself in the bottom of the cool ocean sand. It hides during the day and eats only at night. It is fussy about its diet, which accounts for its distinctive flavor. It travels well and can stay fresh for days out of water. The Greeks and Romans called it the most delicate fish in the world. Its last name is sole, but is has many first names — petrale, Dover, Rex, lemon, gray, etc.

Dover sole is said to be the finest of all the soles in the sea. Here is the way the chefs on the Odyssey treat this delicate friend of gourmets.

6 filets of Dover sole
Salt and pepper to taste
2 Tbs. butter
2 Tbs. lemon juice
1/2 cup white wine
2 egg yolks
1 Tb. tomato paste
1 Tb. cornstarch
1/2 cup sliced boiled shrimps

Rub the filets with salt, pepper, one tablespoon of the butter and one tablespoon of the lemon juice. Put the filets in a baking pan and add the wine. With the remaining butter, spread it over a piece of waxed paper the size of the baking pan and cover. Bake the fish at 325 degrees in the oven for 15 minutes. Pour the pan juices into a bowl. Add the yolks, whisking until smooth. Add the tomato paste, cornstarch, remaining lemon juice and shrimps. Mix well. Put the filets on a serving tray and nap with the sauce. Garnish with boiled potatoes sprinkled with minced parsley. Serves 6.

Scampi Nella Salsa Di Vino

They are white, pink and brown. They have been caught as close as a mile off the shore or as deep as 1,800 feet off the edge of the continental shelf. And they are classified in the United States by how many of them make up a pound. We know them as shrimp.

One female shrimp can lay up to 1,000,000 eggs which hatch in 12 hours. Those shrimp that survive will go through a dozen molts before they become a shrimp as we know them today.

Ever hear of the barber shrimp? This little clever crustacean sets up his business in sea anemones and attracts lines of fish who want to get their fins and scales shaven by the shrimp's razor-like legs.

Shrimp is a six letter word. In Cantonese, it turns up as a two letter word, "ha." Shrimp also turn up in Greek cooking in olive oil and lemon juice; in England, potted; in Denmark, as an open faced sandwich; in Italy, as giant scampi; in Japan, batter fried; in New Orleans, a main ingredient in shrimp bisque and on the Odyssey as:

2 lbs. raw shrimp, shelled and deveined
1/2 cup flour
1/2 cup olive oil
1/2 cup dry white wine
2 tsps. tomato paste
1/4 cup water
1 tsp. salt
1/2 tsp. pepper, freshly ground
Dash of cayenne pepper
1 Tb. parsley, minced
1 scallion, chopped
3 tsps. fresh lemon juice

Wash and drain shrimp. Roll in flour. Heat oil in the skillet, add shrimp and brown on all sides. Drain off oil and reserve. Add wine to the shrimp and cook until wine is absorbed. In another pan mix the reserved oil, tomato paste, water, salt, pepper and cayenne. Cook on low heat for 5 minutes. Pour the sauce over the shrimp. Add parsley and onion and cook another 5 minutes. Top with lemon juice. Serves 6.

Shrimp on a Skewer, Sauce Piquante

One of the classic sauces is Sauce Piquante. The French word "piquante" means prickly, stinging, sharp, tart, etc. And that is just what this sauce is and it marries well with shrimp.

1/3 cup dry white wine
1/3 cup white wine vinegar
1 Tb. chopped shallots
1 cup thick brown stock or demi-glace
1 tsp. chopped parsley
1 tsp. chopped cornichons or spicy pickles
1 tsp. chopped fresh chervil, or 1/4 tsp. dried
1 tsp. chopped fresh tarragon, or 1/4 tsp. dried
36 raw shrimp, peeled and deveined
6 wood skewers

Prepare the sauce by combining the white wine, vinegar and chopped shallots in a non-aluminum saucepan. Reduce the liquid by half. Add brown stock or demi-glace and bring to the boil. Reduce heat and simmer 10 minutes. Just before serving add parsley, cornichons, chervil and tarragon. Broil the shrimp either under a broiler or over charcoal until done, putting six shrimp on each skewer. Brush each skewer with the sauce and pass the sauce separately for those who want more. Serves 6.

SHRIMP

The terror of the tide, the modern "hit man" of shrimpdom, is the pistol shrimp. This demon of the deep has an extra long claw which resembles a pistol. He stuns his prey by noisily snapping it at them.

Sea Bass Apetses Island Style

FISHY SUBJECT

The delicate seasoning of fish is always a tough task for a chef. However there is one herb that has been known as the "fish" herb. It is:

a. Black pepper
b. Dill
c. Fennel
d. White pepper

b. Dill is used in many fish dishes and brings out the subtle taste of fish.

Here is another baked fish dish as served on the Odyssey.

3 lbs. sea bass or white fish
2 lbs. tomatoes, chopped fine
1/2 cup minced parsley
4 cloves garlic, chopped
1 cup olive oil
2 Tbs. lemon juice
1 cup white wine
Salt and pepper to taste

Wash and cut the fish into 8 equal pieces. Put the slices in a well oiled baking dish and cover the slices with the remaining ingredients. Bake 1/2 hour at 250 degrees. Serve the slices separately and cover with the sauce. Serves 8.

Our guide in Cairo

What Shall I Wear?
Formal, Casual or What?

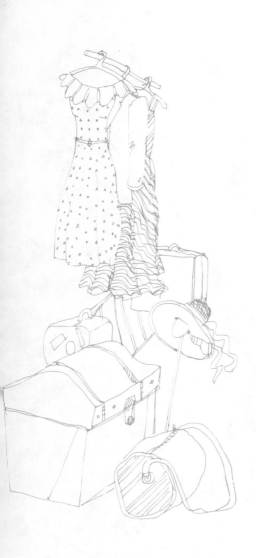

Ok! You've got the tickets, suntan lotion, camera and a list of things Aunt Jane and Uncle Edward want along with several dozen other people.

Now, what do you pack?

Time was when cruising meant Fred Astaire and Ginger Rogers tripping across the ocean on a silver screen in evening dresses and top hat and tails.

Today, informality is the keynote to cruising. But there is still "good taste" that should be observed. For example, swim suits and bare feet are for "deck wear" and not for dining in the lounge.

Here are some suggestions for Odyssey dress.

INFORMAL DINNERS: From 6:00 p.m. on in the lounges and the dining room, ladies usually choose a cocktail dress or an appropriate evening pants ensemble. Gentlemen wear a jacket after 6:00 p.m.; either a sports coat with slacks, tie optional.

FORMAL DINNERS: Such gala affairs as the Captain's Welcome and the Captain's Gala Dinner call for the ladies to wear an evening gown, pants suit, or fancy cocktail dress. For gentlemen, summer light weight evening jacket, a dark suit and necktie or, if one prefers, a tuxedo.

SPECIAL DINNERS AND EVENINGS: On the Odyssey, these special activities are indicated on the daily program along with telling you if it is a "casual, informal or formal" dress day. There is Pastel Night (pink in a variety of hues usually predominates, but anything pastel or almost pastel is in order for both men and women, with men wearing a jacket), Pirate Night (dress casually or piratically if you like!). Then there is Costume Night (depending on your itinerary, it's also called Carnival Night, Byzantine Ball, El Dorado Night) for which passengers often design their own award winning costumes which they wear after dinner. And when in doubt always ask the Odyssey cruise staff what to wear, when and where.

ADDITIONAL SUGGESTIONS: For on board: For women — light daytime dresses, pants, blouses, for knocking around. Bathing suits (three is a good number, so you'll always have a dry one) and coverups for around the pool — or shorts if you prefer. The same goes for men. And don't forget to include a sun block (the sun is stronger than it feels, particularly if a deceptive sea breeze is blowing). Light cotton or polyester materials are perfect for cruising because they don't wrinkle. And tuck in a pair of sandals or two and some sneakers.

For on-shore sight-seeing: For women, sundresses, shorts, light cotton or polyester slacks, short-sleeved shirts, and sandals will suffice for most onshore sightseeing. In some countries, for example, a woman in shorts is frowned upon, or not permitted inside historic churches. (Again, check with the shipboard cruise staff.)

For men, light cotton slacks, shorts, and sport shirts are fine on shore. Bring some comfortable lightweight walking shoes. Sneakers are okay for short walks, but long days of sightseeing may require more arch support.

Lightweight sweaters are always good to have at hand, especially at night, and a raincoat for the unusual inclement weather.

TIP: Non-wrinkly synthetics work best for cruise travel, and they pack into almost nothing.

Last but not least, don't forget a hat! Even with a sunscreen, a hat is the safest protection against sunburn. Native shops in your ports of call always carry straw items, so leave some room in your bag for purchases to bring home.

And remember, have fun!

THE GOOD AMERICAN

Few people realize that once they leave the United States they have automatically become ambassadors. They truly represent the United States in everything they say and do in any foreign country. The secret to being a good American is to listen and learn. The more you listen and learn about the country you are visiting, the more international you become and the more the people of the various countries will look forward to seeing you. If you tell the people in a country you are visiting and that you want to learn about their lifestyle, they will adopt you as a native. And, you will always be welcome.

Cruising the Mediterranean

Fowl

THANKS TOM . . .

One American helped turn the table of early cuisine into palatable cuisine. He was Thomas Jefferson who smuggled rice into America and introduced rice to the Carolinas in 1787, imported Calcutta hogs, introduced waffles, macaroni, French fries and beefsteak to the early American table. He was the first to serve ice cream, French wines, Baked Alaska, Parmesan cheese, almonds, etc.

Chicken is a versatile food. It is good broiled, roasted, baked, steamed, fried, boiled, fricasseed, barbecued, or made into a pie or soup. It has been flavored, stuffed, basted, and garnished with almost every other food, notably, says Waverley Root in his book **Food,** anise, apples, bacon, beans, cinnamon, cornmeal, crabs, crayfish, eels, fennel, ginger, grape jelly, herbs, hickory nuts, lemons, lime juice, maple syrup, marmalade, mushrooms, nutmeg, oranges, oysters, peanut butter, pineapple, sake, sesame seeds, truffles and vinegar.

Man's assocation with the chicken begins some 2,000 B.C. in India, where the wild red jungle fowl was first domesticated. The chicken was initially a sacred bird and priests customarily consumed the remains of sacrificial animals after making offerings of the less edible parts. So the chicken came to the table early in our development.

The chicken traveled to China and on to the Pacific Islands and reached Europe through the Mediterranean about 1500 B.C. The bird shows up in Greece by 720 B.C. It was the Romans who gobbled up chicken around 185 B.C. fattening them up as did the Greeks on the island of Cos. A hundred years later the chicken was firmly established in the kitchens of the world.

Roast Capon Conquistador

In the Odyssey kitchen, fowl is treated with respect so that passengers may enjoy dining on these fat little morsels. One of the most famous dishes aboard the Odyssey is:

1 capon, about 8 lbs.
1 cup lemon juice
Salt and pepper to your taste
2 carrots, sliced thin
1 onion, sliced thin
1/2 cup diced celery
1 cup white wine
2 cups demiglace (or beef stock)
1/2 cup French cognac

Marinate the capon in the lemon juice and salt and pepper for several hours. Put the capon in a deep pot and add the vegetables. Cover and roast 1/2 hour at 250 degrees. Add wine and roast another 1/2 hour. Ten minutes before removing the capon, uncover the pot and let the capon get brown.

Remove the capon from the pot and cut it into serving pieces. Add the demiglace sauce to the pot, stir well and heat the sauce and either pour it over the capon pieces or serve it separately. Serves 6.

HIC!

Herbs play an important part in a chef's menu planning. The ancient Greeks believed that certain herbs could prevent drunkeness. Two of these herbs are:

a. Parsley & Marjoram
b. Garlic & Fennel
c. Caraway & Poppy
d. Coriander & Mint

a. Parsley & Marjoram were woven into wreaths and placed on a drinker's head which was said to prevent the wearer from getting intoxicated.

Village Style Baked Chicken

ODYSSEY QUIZ

Peter The Great drank 21 glasses every morning before gulping down 12 figs and 12 pounds of cherries. Gloria Swanson not only drinks it but bathes in it, and Alice Cooper serves it to his pet boa constructor. It is:

1. Ginger ale
2. Burgundy wine
3. Russian Vodka
4. Bottled water

Give up?

4. Bottled water

Some of the finest cooking in the world comes from the little villages and hamlets of many countries. Here is such a dish, one that has become an Odyssey cruise favorite.

1-3 lb. chicken
juice of two lemons
Salt and pepper to taste
1/2 cup oil
4 chopped scallions
1 tsp. chopped dill
1/2 pound chicken livers
2 tomatoes, peeled, seeded and chopped fine
1/2 pound feta cheese
3 eggs
Pinch of oregano

Leave the chicken whole, marinate it in the lemon juice for a half hour. To make the filling, heat the oil in a casserole dish and add scallions, dill and livers. Cook for 5 minutes. Remove from heat and add remaining ingredients. Blend with hands until well-mixed. Stuff the chicken, tie the legs and roast in a tray in a 250 degree oven for 1 hour, turning every 15 minutes. Serves 6.

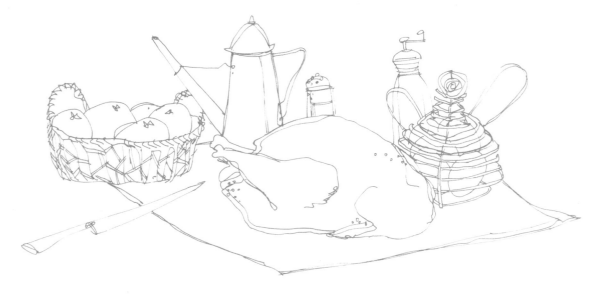

Oregano Chicken

Oregano is an international herb. It is called for as a seasoner in many cuisines and is used in soups, sauces, salads, fish, meats, eggs and cheese, poultry and game, and in vegetables. Here is an excellent example of how chicken and oregano make a delightful dinner feast.

1/2 cup olive oil
3 tsps. salt
4 Tbs. fresh lemon juice
2 4-5 lb. roasting chickens
1/2 cup butter (1 cube)
2 cups canned tomatoes, chopped
1 tsp. pepper, freshly ground
2 tsps. oregano

Combine olive oil, 2 tsp. salt, lemon juice. Rub mixture into chickens, inside and out. Place chickens in roasting pan. Roast in 375 degree oven for 1 hour. In saucepan melt butter. Add tomatoes, 1 tsp. salt, pepper, oregano. Cook and stir over medium heat 5 minutes. Pour mixture over chickens. Reduce oven to 350 degrees. Continue roasting chickens 1 hour more until they are golden brown and tender. Baste frequently. Serves 8.

CHIP OFF THE OLD BLOCK

Do you like potato chips? If you do you can thank an American for having created them. They were originally called "Saratogo chips" because they were created by a chef at the Moon Lake Resort in Saratoga Springs, New York.

The American's name was George Crumb.

He was an American . . . an American Indian.

85

Consomme Caruso

2 whole chicken breasts, skinned and boned
2 slices of white bread
1 whole egg
Salt and pepper to taste
6 cups chicken consomme

Grind the breasts as for hamburger or puree the breasts in a food processor. Dip the bread in water and squeeze dry. Add remaining ingredients, except consomme, and hand mix. If using a food processor add the same ingredients and whirl until well mixed. Shape the mixture into 3/4 inch balls. Poach the balls in water until done, about 15 minutes. Pour the consomme into soup bowls and add 6 balls to each bowl. Serves 6.

Fun in the Sun

Party Time

And you thought you might be bored on a cruise?

Well, not aboard an Odyssey. There is something going on all through the day. And some of the most talked about and colorful events are the various party nights: Pastel Pink Night, Pirate's Night, Greek Night, Costume Ball Night, Famous Couples Cocktail Party, and many more.

Let's look at a few such gala affairs.

Greek Night: Here is where you wear something blue and white which are the colors of the Greek flag. But that night is your night, for the Odyssey crew puts on a colorful show for the passengers. There is dancing, singing and fun. Many of the crew are such professionals that their acting and singing could land them movie contracts. The songs and dances they do are almost 1,000 years old in tradition and have been faithfully reproduced for Odyssey passengers. It is truly a night to remember.

Famous Couples Cocktail Party: Humphrey Bogart has to find Lauren Bacall. Desi Arnaz has to find Lucille Ball and Elizabeth Taylor has to find . . . Well, you get the idea. During this lavish cocktail party, in which all the drinks are paid for by the Captain, you have to find your famous partner. It's a good way for passengers to mingle.

Pirate's Night: "Heave too, me hardies. The buried treasure is near so dig you scum, dig." That's some of the rough and ready language a few people will use at Pirate's Night and they'll be dressed in paper pirate hats, mustaches, bandanas and the most colorful and imaginative costumes will receive prizes direct from a Treasure Chest. HINT: The crew has stashed-away an excellent assortment of novel pirate attire, so don't be afraid to ask them to help you, even if your name isn't Long John Silver.

Pastel Night: Yes, even the menu is printed in pink. There are pink cocktails, pink shrimp and lobster, pink clothes, pink tablecloths, napkins, pink lemonade and pink Champagne. It is a night to think pink (or other soft pastels).

Costume Night: Here's a chance to show how creative you can be. There are prizes for the best and most original costume and the cruise staff has hundreds of ideas. HINT: As long as you know this ahead of time, you can bring along something different for this special night.

White Elephant Auction: Here cruisers auction off everything they don't want or bought on the trip and now decided Aunt Jane probably won't like it. The bidding is fast and there are always a few surprises for everyone.

Lastly, the welcome by the Ship's Captain the first night out is a must. It's a formal affair and more often than not sets the pace of the entire cruise. Do not miss it.

WHAT A PARTY!

In 1476 when the Archbishop of Neville was ordained the feasting went on for several days. The celebrants must have been a hungry lot for they consumed 2,000 geese, 1,000 sheep, 1,000 capons, 4,000 pigeons, 4,000 meat pies, 1,000 jellied dishes, 5,000 deer, and washed this down with 75,600 gallons of wine. They don't toss parties like that anymore.

St. Lucia's Soufriere Harbor

Salads & Vegetables

If you love salads and vegetables, Odyssey cruises are for you.

Salads are one of the oldest of culinary creations. The ancients dined on roots, bulbs, seeds, stems, pods and flowers. Mediterranean people dressed their salads with olive oil or sesame oil, vinegar or lemon juice. The Greeks regarded salads as "food for the gods" and never tossed salads with oil; they "annointed" salads. Romans were extremely fond of lettuce, which they regarded as a sacred plant and often served it last, sprinkled with wine.

In 1390, the cooks to Richard II's kingdom compiled notes explaining that salads were made with parsley, garlic, young onions, leeks, borage, mint, fennel, rue, cresses, rosemary, and dressed with oil, vinegar and salt. (Almost sounds like a 20th Century salad.)

The first book about salads was published in 1699 by John Evelyn. In those days they spelled salad in the English style, "sallets."

Odyssey passengers like salads. The poolside luncheon buffet boasts more than 20 salads everyday and during your cruise, rarely is a salad repeated. While there are many different salads you can enjoy aboard an Odyssey, here are some that you might want to serve your guests after the cruise has ended.

Ukranian Salad

There is no end to one's imagination when it comes to creating salads. The first time I tasted this salad, I was amazed at its taste. I think you will be too.

2 cups white cabbage, shredded
2 cups red cabbage, shredded
1/2 cup onions, minced
1/2 cup sweet pickles, minced
Salt and white pepper to taste
6 Tbs. olive oil or your favorite oil
2 Tbs. red wine vinegar

Put the first four ingredients in a salad bowl. In another bowl, add the remaining ingredients and whisk until well mixed. Take a tablespoon of the dressing at a time and mix it into the greens, tossing to coat them. Add more dressing until you like the mixture. Serves 4.

Brandied Fruit Salad

I am not a fruit salad person. I guess it stems from my days in the U. S. Air Force during WW II when they served the worst fruit combinations doused with some insipid watered down dressings which turned my stomach. However, I have tasted this Odyssey fruit salad and I do admit, I like it.

2 tsps. powdered ginger
1/2 cup brandy
2 oranges, peeled and sliced thin
1 cup pineapple chunks
1 cup strawberries, halved

Dissolve ginger in brandy. Combine fruits in a bowl and baste them with the ginger-brandy mixture. Cover and chill for 3 hours. Serve cold on a bed of crisp lettuce leaves. Serves 4.

93

Aifonat Salad

Sometimes salads take their name from the dressing that they are annointed with, like the world famous Caesar Salad. This is true with the Odyssey's special salad:

Dressing

2 egg yolks
1 cup oil
1/2 cup vinegar
1/2 Tb. Dijon styled mustard
1/2 medium onion, grated
2 cloves garlic, minced
3 Tbs. mayonnaise
Salt and white pepper to taste

Put the above ingredients in a blender or food processor and whirl until well mixed.

For the greens, the Odyssey chefs use a mixture of romaine, endive, celery, escarole, pimento and other greens to make up the salad.

Sliced boiled eggs and feta cheese.

The dressing is poured over the greens, tossed and garnished with the egg slices and sprinkled with the cheese. Serves 6.

Sauerkraut Salad

1 lb. sauerkraut
1 medium onion, chopped fine
1 tsp. sugar
1/2 tsp. fresh ground pepper
4 tsps. salad oil
1 tsp. caraway seeds

Wash sauerkraut under cold water. Dry. Chop fine. Mix remaining ingredients together. Chill. Serve cold on crisp lettuce leaves. Serves 6.

Maziana Carrots

If you are a vegetable gourmet, here's the Odyssey way to serve the best carrots in the world.

1 lb. medium carrots, peeled and cut into sticks
Water
2 Tbs. butter
2 Tbs. honey
Salt and white pepper
Grated nutmeg

Put the carrot sticks in a pan with water to cover and cook until "al dente." Toss with the remaining ingredients. Serve as a garnish or as a vegetable course. Serves 4.

Buttered Squash Puffs

It is too bad that more people do not eat squash. There are so many kinds and varieties that one could plan a menu around the squash family. Here is a great starter.

1 lb. medium sized squash, washed and cut into 1/4 inch
   rounds
2 Tbs. vinegar
1/2 cup flour
2 Tbs. grated cheese, your favorite
Oil for cooking
Salt

Sprinkle the vinegar on the squash rounds. Put the flour on one plate and the grated cheese on another plate. Dip the rounds in the cheese and then the flour. Deep fat fry until crisp. Serves 4.

FROM THE KITCHEN

Cruise people get hungry. Here are just a few of the food items consumed on board.

Prime ribs	900 lbs. per cruise
Tenderloin	1,430 lbs. per cruise
Lobster	550 lbs. per cruise
Milk	1,100 quarts per cruise
Vegetables	500 lbs. daily
Fruits	900 lbs. daily
Eggs	1,440 eggs daily
Rolls	1,600 rolls daily
Butter	80 lbs. daily
Cakes	35 cakes daily
Cookies	200 cookies daily

Cooking and serving that food keeps the chef, his staff of 26 cooks including butchers and bakers, 21 waiters, seven bus boys, two wine stewards and one maitre d'hotel very busy.

95

Stuffed Cabbage

HUNGRY?

In ancient Pompeii, the main meal was taken:

   a. In the morning
   b. At noon
   c. Middle of the late afternoon
   d. After a bath in the early evening

c. This was because the meal lasted so long, often as long as six to eight hours.

Vegetables are an important part of the Odyssey cuisine. They are served in a variety of ways, some traditional and some very creative. Look at an Odyssey's menu and you will taste vegetables the way vegetables should be savored.

1 good-size cabbage
Boiling water
1 lb. pork, ground
1 lb. beef, ground
1 slice bread, soaked in water, crumbled
1 large onion, chopped
1 tsp. salt
1/2 tsp. pepper, freshly ground
1 lb. sauerkraut
3 slices bacon, partly cooked, drained
2 cups tomato juice
1 cup (1/2 pt.) sour cream

Put cabbage in large bowl. Pour boiling water over it. Let stand several minutes. Drain, separate each leaf carefully. Mix ground meats, bread, onion, salt, pepper in bowl. Put 1 tablespoon of mixture in each cabbage leaf, roll up, turning ends in carefully. Put sauerkraut on bottom of earthenware casserole or heavy pot. Carefully arrange cabbage rolls on sauerkraut. Cut bacon slices into three pieces each, place over cabbage rolls. Pour tomato juice over all. Cover, cook gently over medium heat 2 hours. Uncover. Bake 45 minutes in 375 degree oven or until lightly browned. Add sour cream. Heat carefully on top of stove 5 minutes. Serves 4.

Ratatouille Nicoise

As you have read earlier in this book, when a dish has the label "nicoise" it is the cooking of Provence in the south of France. This is one of the wonderful things about the cuisine of the Odyssey ships: they serve an international cuisine.

1/3 cup olive oil
2 cloves garlic, minced
1 large onion, sliced
2 medium zucchini, scrubbed
1 small eggplant
3 Tbs. flour
2 green peppers, seeded, cut in strips
4 big tomatoes, peeled and sliced
1 tsp. salt
1/2 tsp. pepper, freshly ground
1 Tb. capers

In large skillet, heat oil. Add garlic and onion, cook gently until onion is transparent. Slice zucchini. Peel and cube eggplant. Lightly flour all pieces and add with green peppers to skillet. Cover. Cook slowly 1 hour. Add tomatoes, continue to simmer uncovered until mixture is thick like stew. Season with salt and pepper. Add capers last 15 minutes of cooking. Serves 6.

WAGES

Chefs today are still one of the underpaid people of the world. Of course they are better off than chefs in Merry Olde England. During the Renaissance period, cooks, as they were called then, only received about $12.00 per year for wages. And then they usually put in a 16 hour day for the pittance they were paid.

Oven Potatoes "Lemonato"

Someone once said that there are as many ways to serve potatoes as there are potatoes. Just a few weeks ago I saw a story in a national women's magazine about 20 new ways to serve potatoes and the only difference was 20 different toppings.

Aboard an Odyssey, potatoes are served in a variety of ways. Like this recipe for example:

2 lbs. potatoes, peeled, washed and cut into quarters
4 cloves garlic, sliced very thin
1/2 cup lemon juice
1 cup water
Salt and pepper to taste

Put the potatoes in a roasting pan and sprinkle with the remaining ingredients. Bake in a 250 degree oven for 45 minutes, or until the potatoes are brown. Serve as an accompaniment to roast meats or steak. Serves 6.

Pont Neuf Potatoes a la Padre

Here is a different way to serve potatoes which come out light and tasty.

1 lb. large potatoes, peeled
1 pint oil
Salt to taste

Cut potatoes into 1/2 inch sticks, with all sides even. Heat the oil in a deep pan and when the oil is bubbling, dip the potatoes into the oil and cook about 30 to 60 seconds, depending upon how many potatoes you cook in one batch. Sprinkle with salt. Serves 6.

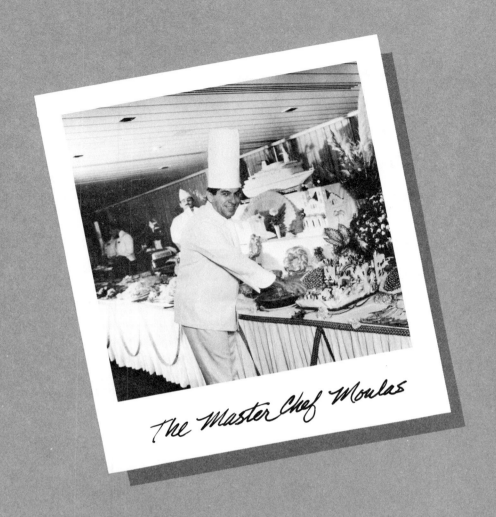

The Master Chef Moulas

The Top People
And What They Do

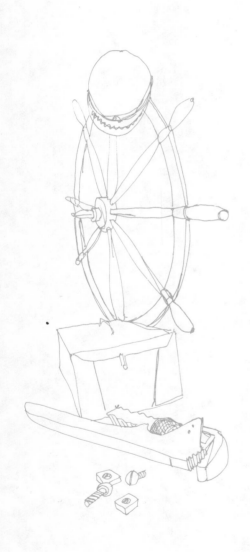

"Auntie Jane," the little girl said, "what does the Captain do?"

The elderly lady in the purple dress looked down at her seven year old niece and said, "Steer the ship, my dear, steer the ship."

Have you often wondered just what all those people aboard ship do?

Here's a quick rundown on the ship's top personnel, the men and women who keep Odyssey passengers happy on their cruise.

THE CAPTAIN

He is the overall master of the ship. All senior officers report to him. He makes all the major decisions relating to passenger safety. While often portrayed as the social father image to the passengers by Hollywood movies and television shows, this does not reflect his true and larger responsibility for the ship, its crew and passengers. He is like a god on his little floating island . . . all activities, even the time of day, are ultimately set by him.

STAFF CAPTAIN

Second in charge, but primary responsibility is over all the ship's crew, particularly the deck and engine departments.

PURSER

He is responsible for all financial matters for the ship, payment of all ship's crew salaries, collection of funds due from passengers for shipboard accounts, maintaining safe deposit boxes. His department also handles all matters with the port and immigration authorities.

CHIEF ENGINEER

Responsible for all the mechanical and electrical, et cetera equipment on board including the refrigeration equipment for the air conditioning and the freezers for the food, the heating systems for the cabins and the power plant to move the ship itself.

CRUISE DIRECTOR

The Cruise Director and his cruise staff are responsible for all the social activities on board. The scheduling of parties, evening entertainment, afternoon deck games, bingo, bridge and galley tours and generally the shore excursions at each port come from the Cruise Office. The entertainers on board report to the Cruise Director. He is the producer and director of the activities on board.

DOCTOR

He is responsible for the medical attention and health of all the passengers and the crew. In the case of a Greek ship, he must speak Greek as the 200 to 300 crew members on board are Greek nationals.

ENTERTAINERS

As the name implies, the ship carries a team of people to provide entertainment for the passengers. Bands, singers, magicians, puppeteers, et cetera are on staff.

CHIEF STEWARD

All the hotel service staff report to him. All the cabin service, dining room service and public room service fall in this category. Any questions about the staterooms should be brought to him.

MAITRE D'

This gentleman is in charge of the dining room. The head waiters report to him. Any questions about food service should be directed to him or one of his head waiters.

The Royal Odyssey

Desserts

The whole world has a sweet tooth. And you and I love it.

We are all born with a sweet tooth, and that is why mother's milk tastes better than formula milk. Our sweet tooth is why we all like desserts in one form or another.

The desserts aboard an Odyssey are varied to suit the palates of the thousands of passengers Royal Cruise Line hosts. They range from the cool, simple and pleasureable offerings to the rich, sublime and decadent taste treats.

Some years ago when I was in the south of France, I visited the young chef Michel Guerard, whose restaurant and spa has earned him 3 ★ ★ ★ in the Michelin Guide. We sat in the lounge, Michel, his lovely wife, Christine, my wife Yvonne and our mutual friend, Robert Garrapit, chef de cuisine, l'Europe Villeneuve de Marsan, who recently obtained 1 ★.

The subject was desserts and we all agreed that the new light desserts were just the thing for everyone. And so it is aboard an Odyssey with a special ice cold dessert:

Cube of Pineapple, Creme de Menthe

If you like simple desserts and are especially fond of fruit, the Odyssey chefs offer this with little calories and a lot of flavor.

1 large pineapple, peeled and cut into quarters
8 Tbs. green creme de menthe

Pour 2 Tbs. of the creme de menthe over each one of the pineapple quarters. Serves 4.

Almond Puff Pastry

And if in the evening you like something sweet to nibble on with a glass of pale cream sherry, the Odyssey chefs suggest the following:

1 cup water
1/4 lb. butter (1 stick)
1 cup sugar
1 tsp. almond extract
2 cups flour, sifted
1/4 cup blanched almonds

Preheat oven to 325 degrees. In saucepan combine water, butter, sugar, almond extract. Bring to a boil, then cook gently until butter and sugar are thoroughly melted. Add flour all at once. Beat vigorously. Cook over low heat 5 minutes, beating constantly. Spread pastry on greased 10 x 15-inch jelly roll pan, or in two 8 inch square pans. Cut in diamonds with sharp knife. Put an almond in center of each piece. Bake 15 minutes, then run under broiler for a minute, just long enough to brown the top. Yield: 24 - 36 diamonds.

Chocolate Mousse

I have to admit that chocolate mousse is one of my very favorite desserts. And I suspect just about everyone has their own favorite recipe. Here is the Odyssey favorite.

2 Tbs. cold coffee
3 oz. sweet chocolate
4 egg yolks
1 cup sugar
4 egg whites
1-1/2 cups whipping cream

Combine coffee and chocolate and heat slowly until the chocolate is melted. Cool 15 minutes. Beat yolks until light in color. Add sugar and whisk until fluffy. Add cooled chocolate. Beat whites until stiff. Fold into chocolate mixture. Whip cream and fold into mixture. Pour into 2 quart mold and chill 4 hours. Serves 8.

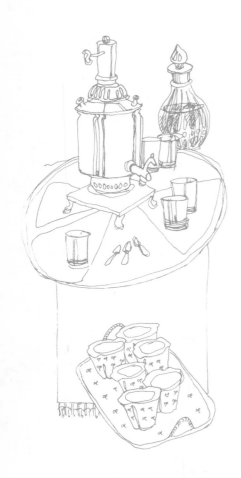

Champagne Sorbet

1 cup Champagne
2 cups water
3/4 cup sugar

Mix together and put into an ice cream machine until it thickens, or chill overnight in the freezer compartment of your freezer. Serves 4.

Walnut Pancakes

I don't know why more people do not serve pancakes as a dessert. I guess it was because in the early days, our founding fathers liked something sweet in the morning, something solid enough to get them through to lunchtime. But here is a light pancake dessert, just right for closing the curtain on a fine dinner.

2 eggs plus 1 egg yolk
1/2 cup sugar
2 tsps. lemon rind, grated
3/4 cup walnuts, ground fine
3 Tbs. flour, sifted
3 Tbs. brandy
1/4 lb. butter (1 stick)
1/4 cup confectioners' sugar, sifted

In a bowl, beat eggs and egg yolk. Add sugar gradually, beating until light. Add lemon rind, nuts, flour. Beat until well blended. Add brandy. Mix. Melt half the butter, add to batter and mix gently.

TO BAKE: In a 7-inch skillet, melt small piece of remaining butter. Pour 1 Tbs. batter into it. Turn pan back and forth to coat bottom. Make pancakes as thin as possible. Cook over low heat until golden brown on both sides. Remove from skillet. Roll up immediately. Repeat until all batter is used. Sprinkle with powdered sugar. Yield: 36 medium sized pancakes.

Crepes Suzette

It was Henri Charpentier who created Crepes Suzette, probably the most famous of all crepe recipes. He was just 15 when he first served this dish at the Cafe de Paris in Monte Carlo. He was one of the assistant waiters and often helped Edward, The Prince of Wales choose a menu. One morning he bragged to the Prince, who was known for his exceptional palate, that the Prince would taste a sweet never before served to anyone.

This was quite a boast for a lad of 15 but with true French breeding and a bit of arrogance, little Henri was about to make a name for himself that the world would never forget.

Everything was going along perfectly, when suddenly the cordials and liqueurs caught fire.

Was he ruined? How was he to begin all over, especially in front of one of Europe's great gastronomes?

He tasted the sauce and knew now he had won the victory. Like a true chef that he was later to become, Henri slowly folded the crepes into the sweet sauce, turning them over and over so that would absorb just enough of the sauce.

As he turned he was inspired again and added more liqueurs and flamed them. When the flames had died he served them to the Prince and his party, which included a little girl.

The Prince obviously enjoyed them for he used his spoon to scoop up the last remaining ounces of the special sweet sauce.   The Prince asked Henri what his new creation was called and he replied "Crepe Princess." Because of the young lady present the Prince asked Henri to change the name to Crepes Suzette, and he did.

Crepes Suzette (cont.)

1/4 lb. butter, melted
1/2 cup of sugar
Grated rind of 1 orange
Grated rind of 1 lemon
Juice of 1 lemon
Juice of 1 orange
3 ounces of brandy
3 ounces of Cointreau
12 dessert crepes

Melt the butter in a chafing dish. Add sugar, orange and lemon rind and cook the mixture until it carmelizes. One by one pass each crepe through the mixture until well coated. Four-fold the crepes and push them to one side of the chafing dish. Add orange and lemon juice, brandy and Cointreau to the chafing dish. When heated, ignite spooning the flaming liquid over the crepes until the flame dies out.

Cherries Jubilee

Here is one of the oldest flaming desserts in the world.

1 pint Bing Cherries, plus juice
1/2 tsp. cornstarch
1 Tbs. water
2 oz. Kirsch
Vanilla ice cream

Pour the juice into a chafing dish. Place the pan over the heat and bring the cherry juice to the boil. Mix the cornstarch and water and add it to the chafing dish. Add the cherries. In a separate pan heat the Kirsch until it sizzles. Ignite and pour over cherries. When the flame dies, pour some of the cherries and sauce over a portion of vanilla ice cream. Serves 4.

TEA TIME

If you are a tea drinker you should know that teas are graded according to the age of the leaves used. The best grade is orange pekoe, made from the newest, youngest leaves and terminal buds. Lower grades, in descending order, are pekoe, pekoe Souchong and Souchong.

109

Baked Alaska Flambee

ANOTHER FIRST

Eighty percent of the French Champagne is consumed by the:

a. English
b. Germans
c. French
d. Russians
e. Americans
f. None of the above

c. The French know a good drink when they taste it.

People often ask me how they can flame dishes at home and have the brandy or liqueur ignite. The simple trick is to make sure that whatever spirit you use, that spirit is heated to the point where little bubbles start rising from the bottom of the pan to the top of the liquid. This is known as the "sizzle." When the spirit reaches this point, the alcohol is evaporating and is ready to be ignited. This is the only fool-proof method I know that works every time and all the time.

1 qt. Neapolitan ice cream
6 egg whites
6 Tbs. confectioner's sugar
Wooden board
1 sheet plain white paper
1 inch slice of pound or sponge cake

Freeze the ice cream in a freezer until it is very hard, about 4 to 6 hours. Beat the whites and add the sugar. The whites are ready when they hold their peaks. Put the white paper on the wooden board. Add the cake and place the ice cream on top of the cake. Spread the whites evenly on all sides and top of the ice cream. Bake in a 400 degree oven until the whites get slightly brown. With a sharp knife, cut the Baked Alaska into eight portions. Serves 8.

NOTE: To flame the Baked Alaska, do not cut it. Heat in a pan 1/4 cup California brandy until it sizzles. Put the Baked Alaska on a platter slightly larger than the Baked Alaska. When the brandy is very hot, ignite it and pour the flaming mixture around the cake and bring it to the table flaming. When the flame dies, cut the cake and spoon some of the brandy over the cake.

The Islands of Greece

How To Become A Wine Expert

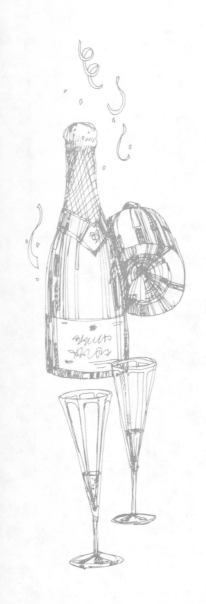

Do the words bouquet, body and acid bother you? Are you at a loss for words when someone at the dinner table asks you what you think of the aroma of the wine you have just tasted? And do you have trouble picking out a wine or wines to match the various courses you have selected?

If so, the Golden Odyssey and Royal Odyssey have come to the rescue with their "Wine Seminars At Sea". This unique program lets all Odyssey passengers participate in three one and a half hour seminars during each of the seventeen winter cruises of the Panama Canal or the Caribbean. The pilot program was kicked off by Daniel Mirassou, President of the Mirassou Vineyards, San Jose. The seminar was so popular that other California wine experts have been asked to participate. In the future such experts will include Eric Wente, President, Wente Bros., James McManus, President, California Brandy Advisory Board, Jan Wells, Vice-President, Paul Masson Vineyards, Tom Wigginton, President, Franciscan Vineyards, Louis Martini, President, Louis M. Martini Vineyards, John Wright, President, Domaine Chandon, and many others.

"The object of this seminar," says Daniel Mirassou, "is to help people enjoy various wines, to make judgments as to what wines they like and to marry them with the various foods offered aboard the ship."

"Even though many of the seminar attendees, which is about half the passengers on the ship, drank wine perhaps two or three times a week, they didn't know that much about wines. They learned something about wines for the first time and they found out that it was fun."

"We started off with Champagne at the first day's seminar," Daniel said, "and of course that was very popular. More and more people are drinking Champagne today and so naturally there was a great deal of interest."

Daniel went on to explain how the participants learned about the different ways producers make Champagne; the charmat, the transfer method and the methode champenoise. Participants were allowed to taste the three Champagnes which reflected the three methods and make their judgments. In addition, participants tasted a French champagne, made by the methode champenoise just to taste

the difference since the grapes are dissimilar and the composition of the soil is not the same. Moreover, each Champagne house in the United States as well as France has their own secret method of blending various Champagnes to appeal to their customers' tastes, and this must be taken into consideration when tasting Champagnes

"We also talked about yeasts in making Champagne, which they were very much interested in because different yeasts can produce different tasting Champagnes," he added.

The second and third days were devoted to tasting white wines like Vouvary, Chablis, Chenin Blanc and Johannisberg Riesling and red wines such as Beaujolais, Bordeaux and Cabernet Sauvignon. Such a wide range of wines to taste broadens the participants knowledge of wines.

"I also like to mention the various kinds of foods that these wines will marry with," Daniel said. "And we have made suggestions to the Odyssey's chief steward about which wines would match his menus."

On the last day of the seminar, Daniel presented the 250 plus attendees with a Certificate of Wine Appreciation, acknowledging their expertise in the world of wine.

"What I have tried to do," says Daniel, "is to give the people an overall view of wines; how to open them, when to use a decanter, temperature of wines, foods and wines, breathing of wines, special occasions for wines; all these are important along with tasting the different wines."

WHO WAS FIRST?

Chenin Blanc came on the market in California about 25 years ago. The first winery to make and market this delicious wine was:

1. Ernest and Julio Gallo
2. Louis Martini
3. Beaulieu Vineyards
4. Charles Krug

Give up?

4. Charles Krug

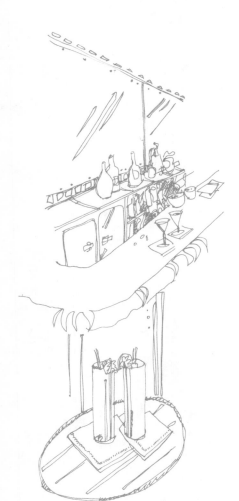

He can remember your name, the kind of drink you like and if you preferred a lime or lemon twist. Every drink must be perfect. He is a man of talent, precision, daring and delight.

And he is internationally known for his awesome and faultless "four foot pour", a spectacular arch of a beverage cascading from above his head into a tiny 1-1/2 ounce jigger.

His name is Theo and he has been the bartender in the Golden Odyssey's Wooden Horse for more than 200 cruises. People seek him out and order their favorite drink.

Under stress of preparing for VIP parties, special events, the Captain's affairs, Theo never loses his cool. The pleasure of his customer is his first concern. Every drink must be perfect. He has a keen memory, and remembers each guest's favorite libation. He keeps impeccable records. Bartending is his business. He does it extremely well.

Here are four of Theo's great drinks, ones you can duplicate at home to bring back those Odyssey memories.

Calypso Planter's Punch

Juice 1 lime
Juice 1/2 lemon
Juice 1/2 orange
2 tsp. pineapple juice
2 oz. dark rum
Dash Triple Sec

Mix fruit juices in a collins glass filled with ice. Stir until glass is frosted. Add rum, stir and top with Triple Sec. Decorate with orange slice and fresh mint sprig dipped in powdered sugar. Serve with a straw. Makes one.

Theo's Piña Colada

3 oz. rum
4 Tbs. coconut milk
3 Tbs. crushed, fresh pineapple
2 cups crushed ice

Blend at high speed and strain into tall stemmed glass. Garnish with fresh pineapple wedge. Makes one.

Crazy Horse Mai-Tai

1/2 tsp. powdered sugar
2 oz. dark Jamaican Rum
1 oz. Triple Sec
1 Tbs. Grenadine
1 Tbs. Lime Juice

Combine ingredients in a shaker with ice and strain into large old-fashioned glass about 1/3 full of crushed ice. Garnish with maraschino cherry and fresh pineapple wedge. Serve with short straws. Makes one.

Odyssey Ramos Fizz

1 egg white
1 tsp. powered sugar
2 oz. dry gin
Juice of 1/2 lemon
1 Tbs. heavy cream
Dash orange flower water

Shake with ice and strain into a stemmed wine or claret glass. Fill with carbonated water. Makes one.

"POP" GOES THE PIPER

If you are a wine lover you will never go thirsty aboard the Royal Odyssey. It carries the following

White Wines	18,000 bottles
Red Wines	9,000 bottles
Rose	3,600 bottles
Champagnes & Sparkling Wines	5,400 bottles
Sweet Wines	900 bottles

Salut!!

The beauty of Norway's Fjords

Closing The Curtain

It is the last night before your Odyssey slips into its final port. There are things, places, people, food, wines, sights, friendships and memories you store away only to recall in those private moments when someone mentions a cruise.

Everyone has his or her personal adventures, relics of an out-of-the-ordinary experience, a memory, something to write about, a very special entry in a journal or diary, a magic that you can never replace, a part of your life forever.

There's a special magic once you leave the ship. It seems to linger over you; it is in all your thoughts and words and actions.

You constantly tell people about the ship, the food and the places you have visited. And you even embellish them a little bit because of your enthusiasm for the cruise.

For everytime you see a picture of a ship in the newspaper travel section, you will recall your own trip.

And everytime someone mentions their trip, you are ready to tell them about yours.

And all the friends and relatives will help you remember the trip everytime they thank you for their gifts.

Someday soon, the haunting cry of Davey Jones·locker will call you back to the sea. You'll find yourself standing on the deck of your cruise ship, the ship's horn signalling its departure, and the giant ship slowly pulling away from the dock.

You are off to new places and new adventures. There is only one thing left to say:

North African Lemon Dressing

Here are a few extra recipes that you can use to brighten your table presentations.

2 lemons
1-1/2 tsp. salt
1/8 tsp. cayenne pepper
2 cloves garlic, minced
2/3 cup olive oil
1/2 tsp. each coriander, cumin, dry mustard
2 tsp. sugar
1/2 tsp. paprika

Grate lemons, save peel. Squeeze 1/4 cup lemon juice. In a jar with a tight-fitting lid, combine peel and lemon juice with all remaining ingredients. Shake well to blend. Refrigerate. Shake again before using. Yield: 1 cup. Use for fruit salads.

Pepper Cream Dressing

Here is an excellent pepper cream dressing for your favorite salad greens.

2 cups mayonnaise
1-1/2 tsp. ground pepper
1 Tb. lemon juice
1/2 tsp. hot sauce
1 Tb. Worcestershire sauce
3/4 cup water
3 Tbs. grated Parmesan cheese

Put everything into a blender and whirl for one minute or until well mixed. Serves 6.

Tiropites

I am using my imagination when preparing these golden-crisp pastries. A variety of Greek cheeses can be used for the fillings. This recipe uses feta cheese, which you should find in the delicatessen section of most American supermarkets — along with the thin Greek filo pastry.

(Savory Cheese Triangles)
1 8-oz. package cream cheese
1/2 lb. feta cheese, crumbled
2 eggs, slightly beaten
1 Tb. all-purpose flour
Pinch of salt, if desired
1 tsp. ground nutmeg
1/2 lb. plus 3 Tbs. butter or margarine, melted
1 lb. commercial filo pastry sheets, cut into thirds (3 by 11 inches)

In a bowl, combine cheese, eggs, flour, salt (omit salt if feta is very salty), nutmeg and 3 Tbs. butter. Cover bowl. Chill several hours or overnight. Take out of refrigerator 1 hour before using.

Pile up filo, cover with waxed paper and damp towel. Take out 1 sheet. Keep rest covered. Butter filo, using pastry brush and 1/2 lb. butter or margarine, melted and warm. Put 1 teaspoon filling 1 inch from end nearest you. Fold filo back over filling so bottom edge meets left edge, making a right angle. Keep folding back at right angles to make triangular shape with each sheet of filo. (See illustration.) Repeat this procedure. Place on baking sheets and keep covered until all are ready to bake. Bake at 350 degrees for 20-25 minutes or until golden and crisp, turning once. Serve hot. Makes about 60 triangles (2-1/2 inches).

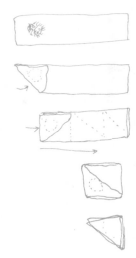

Melitzanosalaya

(Eggplant Salad)
1 large eggplant (about 1-1/2 lbs.)
1 clove garlic
1/4 cup olive oil
2 Tbs. snipped parsley
1 large tomato, diced
1 Tb. grated onion
1 tsp. oregano, crumbled
3 Tbs. white wine vinegar
Salt and freshly ground pepper

Preheat oven to 350 degrees. Bake eggplant 1 hour. Let cook. Peel and dice in 1/2 inch cubes. Split garlic, rub salad bowl with cut side. Discard garlic. Pour olive oil into salad bowl, sprinkle with salt and pepper. Add eggplant, parsley, tomato, onion and oregano. Pour vinegar over vegetables. Mix thoroughly. Season with salt and pepper to taste. Chill thoroughly. Toss lightly just before serving. Serves 4.

Spaghetti a la Carbonero

3 ounces butter
4 eggs
3 ounces grated parmesan cheese
2 pounds cooked spaghetti
3 ounces bacon, chopped and sauteed
3 ounces heavy cream (whipping cream)
White pepper
Dash of salt

Cream the butter until soft and fluffy and set aside. Beat the eggs until very light, add the parmesan cheese, blend well and set aside. Drain the freshly boiled pasta into a heated serving bowl, add the butter and toss until well blended. Add the bacon, the hot cream, the beaten eggs and the cheese mixture, blending together thoroughly. The heat of the pasta and cream should cook the raw eggs on contact. Season with salt and pepper to taste and serve at once. Serves 8.

Moussaka

LOOKING FOR A GOOD WHITE SAUCE . . .

BECHAMEL

A simple combination of butter, flour and milk commonly known as "white sauce"

1/3 cup butter
1/3 cup flour
3 cups hot milk
1 tsp. salt
Dash of white pepper
Dash of nutmeg, if desired

Melt butter in saucepan. Add flour, stirring with a fork to mix. Add hot milk and seasoning, stirring vigorously. Cook gently 25 to 30 minutes. Keep stirring until sauce is thick and smooth, then occasionally for remaining time. Strain. If sauce is not to be used immediately, stir occasionally as it cools to prevent crust from forming on top.

(Greek Eggplant Casserole)
8 Tbs. olive oil
1 medium onion, chopped
1-1/2 lbs. ground lean lamb or beef
1/2 cup dry white wine
1-1/2 cups chopped tomatoes
Salt
Freshly ground pepper
4 Tbs. snipped parsley
1/4 tsp. oregano
1/2 cup bread crumbs
2 eggs, separated
3 medium eggplant
3 cups medium white sauce
1 cup sharp cheddar cheese, shredded
Ground nutmeg

In 2 tablespoons hot oil saute onion until soft and golden. Stir in ground meat. Simmer 4-5 minutes. Stirring constantly, add wine, tomatoes, herbs, salt, pepper. Cover, simmer 30 minutes. Cool. Add egg whites and 2 tablespoons bread crumbs. Blend thoroughly with spoon.

Pare eggplant, cut off green top. Cut in slices 1/2 inch thick. Salt, rinse, dry slices. Fry lightly on both sides in remaining hot olive oil. Use more if necessary to keep from sticking Drain.

Into white sauce stir egg yolks and half the grated cheese. Mix well. Butter a 9 x 12 x 2 inch baking pan. Sprinkle lightly with bread crumbs. Line bottom of pan with half the eggplant slices, cover completely with meat mixture. Layer on remaining eggplant. Pour sauce over all. Sprinkle with nutmeg, remaining cheese and bread crumbs. Bake at 350 degrees for 35-40 minutes or until top crust is golden brown. Let set 10 minutes. Serve warm and cut in squares. Serves 8.

Greek Salad

1 qt. chilled crisp salad greens, torn into bite-size pieces
4-8 radish "roses"
8 large black olives
1 red onion, peeled and sliced into thin rings
1 small green pepper, seeded and cut into thin rings
4-8 tomato wedges or cherry tomatoes
4-8 flat anchovy fillets
Salt to taste
1 clove garlic, peeled and split
Freshly ground pepper to taste
3 Tbs. lemon juice or white wine vinegar
9-11 Tbs. olive oil

Into salad bowl pour a small amount of salt (which traditionally could be sea salt) and rub well into surface with cut garlic. Add crisp greens and all other salad ingredients. Sprinkle with lemon juice or vinegar, toss lightly. Add oil, toss again. Correct amount of oil, lemon juice or vinegar to taste. Serve immediately. Makes 4 to 6 servings.

SAUCE FOR THE GOOSE . . .

In Shakespeare's time, the most widely used sauces were parsley sauce and creamed garlic sauce. There were other sauces in Elizabethan cooking, but for most people it was enough to splash a large amount of vinegar on meat, chicken and fish. And today, vinegar is still one of the most popular flavor enhancers.

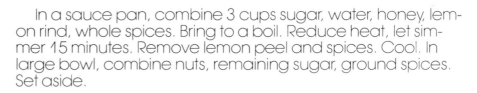

Baklava

(Festive Greek Pastry)

3 1/2 cups sugar
2 1/2 cups water
2 Tbs. honey
Rine of 1 lemon
1 stick cinnamon
4 whole cloves
1 1/2 lbs. combined shelled walnuts and almonds, chopped medium fine
2 Tsp. ground cloves
1 1/2 lbs. commercial filo pastry sheets
1 lb. sweet butter, melted

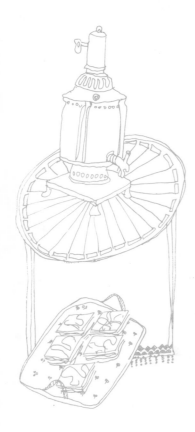

In a sauce pan, combine 3 cups sugar, water, honey, lemon rind, whole spices. Bring to a boil. Reduce heat, let simmer 15 minutes. Remove lemon peel and spices. Cool. In large bowl, combine nuts, remaining sugar, ground spices. Set aside.

Lay filo sheets flat. Cover with waxed paper and damp towel. Keep covered. Count out 8 filo sheets, fold, cover, refrigerate for top. With pastry brush, butter 11-1/2 x 15 x 3 inch baking pan. Lay 1 filo sheet on bottom, brush with warm butter. Butter and stack 8 more sheets on top. Scoop up handful nut-spice mixture. Sprinkle evenly over top filo sheet in pan. Lay on 3 more buttered filo sheets. Again sprinkle nut mixture evenly over top. Continue until all nuts and filo are used. Remove sheets from refrigerator and brush each with butter. Lay over top of all.

With a long, sharp knife score the baklava from top to bottom into diamond shapes of any size desired. Be sure knife touches bottom of pan. Heat remaining butter to sizzling; pour over top. Bake in 300 degree oven for 1-1/2 hours or until light golden in color and flaky. Remove pan to rack. Spoon cooled syrup over entire pastry. Cool in pan. Serve each piece individually. Makes up to 60 to 70 "diamonds."

And so like all good things, your cruise is over. The memories will never fade, they will only get stronger. And they will tease and taunt you into that next cruise. Before long you will be at sea again, aboard an Odyssey, to enjoy and relax under the sun.

See you on the next cruise!

Bon Voyage.

Alphabet of Flags

An International Method of Sea Communication

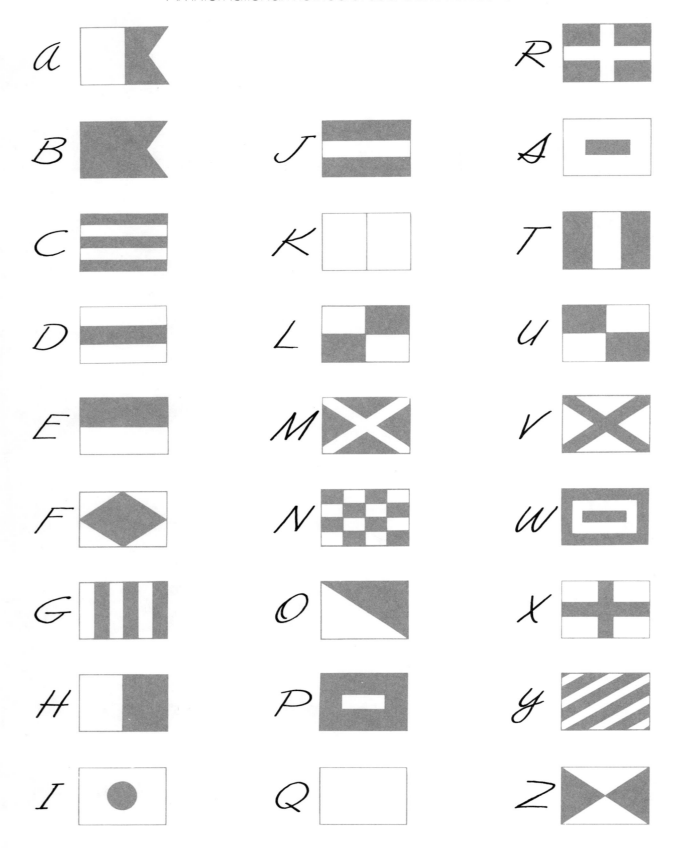

INDEX